Sex and Sex Education

WHAT DO WE TELL OUR CHILDREN?

© The International Institute of Islamic Thought, 1435AH / 2014CE

The International Institute of Islamic Thought
P.O. Box 669, Herndon, VA 20172, USA
www.iiit.org

London Office
P.O. Box 126, Richmond, Surrey, TW9 2UD, UK
www.iiituk.com

ISBN 978-1-56564-570-7

The views and opinions expressed in this book are those of the contributors and not necessarily those of the publisher. The publisher, writers, editors or individuals who have contributed to this publication do not assume any legal liability or responsibility for the use, application of, and/or reference to opinions, findings, conclusions, or recommendations included in this publication. The publisher is not responsible for the information provided and claims for damages caused by the use of any information will therefore be rejected. The publisher is not responsible for use of objects such as images, graphics, or texts from other electronic or printed publications. While every effort has been made to make the information presented in this book as complete and accurate as possible, the publisher is not responsible for the accuracy of information presented, or for URLs for external or third-party internet websites referred to in this publication, and does not guarantee that any content on such websites is, or will remain, accurate or appropriate.

Typesetting and cover design by Ian Abdallateef Whiteman
Illustrations and picture research by Hanna Whiteman

Images © iStockphoto

Printed by Gutenberg Press Ltd, Malta

The Authors

Hisham Yahya Altalib

Dr. Hisham Yahya Altalib was born in Mosul, Nineva, Iraq in 1940. He holds a B.Sc. in electrical engineering from Liverpool University (1962) and a Ph.D. in electrical engineering from Purdue University in Lafayette, Indiana, USA (1974).

During his employment as an electrical engineer, Dr. Altalib soon became active in Islamic work in North America, which continues to this day. He has held several positions in various Islamic organizations, including first full-time director of the Leadership Training Department of the Muslim Students Association of the United States and Canada (MSA) (1975–1977) and secretary general of the International Islamic Federation of Student Organizations (IIFSO) in 1976. He has conducted many training camps and seminars in America and abroad.

A founding member and Director of the SAAR Foundation (1983–1995), as well as founding member of the International Institute of Islamic Thought (IIIT) in 1981, he is also the author of *Mithāq al-Sharaf al-Da'awy* (Arabic) and the well-known book *A Training Guide for Islamic Workers*, which to date has been translated into over 20 languages. He is currently the director of finance of the IIIT.

He is a father and a grandfather.

AbdulHamid Ahmad AbuSulayman

Dr. AbdulHamid Ahmad AbuSulayman was born in Makkah in 1936, where he completed his high school education. He holds a B.A. in commerce from the University of Cairo (1959), an M.A. in Political Science from the University of Cairo (1963), and a Ph.D. in International Relations from the University of Pennsylvania (1973).

He has held various positions throughout his career, including secretary for the State Planning Committee, Saudi Arabia (1963–1964); founding member of the Association of Muslim Social Scientists (AMSS) (1972); secretary general of the World Assembly of Muslim Youth (WAMY) (1973–1979); chairman, Department of Political Science at King Saud University, Riyadh, Saudi Arabia (1982–1984); and Rector of the International Islamic University (IIU), Malaysia (1988–1998).

Instrumental in organizing many international academic conferences and seminars, Dr. AbuSulayman is currently the president of the International Institute of Islamic Thought (IIIT) and author of many articles and books on reforming Muslim societies, including *The Islamic Theory of International Relations: New Directions for Islamic Methodology and Thought*; *Crisis in the Muslim Mind*; *Marital Discord: Recapturing the Full Islamic Spirit of Human Dignity*; *Revitalizing Higher Education in the Muslim World* and *The Qur'anic Worldview: A Springboard for Cultural Reform.*

He is a father and a grandfather.

Omar Hisham Altalib

Dr. Omar Hisham Altalib was born in Kirkuk, Iraq in 1967 and left to the USA with his parents in 1968. He graduated from George Mason University in 1989 with a B.A. in Economics and a B.A. in Sociology and holds an M.A. (1993) and a Ph.D. (2004) in Sociology from the University of Chicago. He was granted a Graduate Student Fellowship from the National Science Foundation (1989–1992) and became an Adjunct Professor of Sociology at Daley College, Chicago (1998) and at Indiana University Northwest, Gary, Indiana (1999).

He was an Assistant Professor of Sociology and Criminology at Ashland University, Ohio (2000–2003) and served as Senior Knowledge Engineer at Science Applications International Corporation at Alexandria, Virginia (2005–2006). He was Assistant Professor of Sociology at the International Islamic University, Malaysia (2009–2011). Dr. Altalib has authored several articles on the family, education, endowments, charitable organizations and social work. He frequently attends academic conferences and travels worldwide.

Acknowledgements

What a blessing it was when the Board of Trustees of the International Institute of Islamic Thought (IIIT) decided to entrust the authors with the great responsibility of writing this work.

To Dr. Ahmad Totonji, Dr. Fathi Malkawi, Dr. Jamal Barzinji, and Dr. Yaqub Mirza, we offer our heartfelt thanks for keeping the wheels of IIIT in motion while we worked on the completion of this book.

We offer our gratitude to the reviewers who offered valuable suggestions for improving the text, particularly Batoul Tu'mah, Zainab Alawi, Michèle Messaoudi, Wanda Krause, Maida Malik, Sara Mirza and Gasser Auda. To Dr. Iqbal Unus who reviewed the first table of contents. To Lina Malkawi and Zeena Altalib who prepared and formatted the initial artwork and made valuable contributions to the manuscript.

Our thanks also go to:

Akbar Ali Mir, Ashraf Sabrin, Saif Altalib, Zaid Altalib, Noha Altalib and Mahmoud Sherif who typed and copied several drafts of the book.

Dr. Tanveer Mirza and Salma Ashmawi, who provided real life examples through the parenting workshops held at ADAMS (All Dulles Area Muslim Society) in Herndon, Virginia, USA.

Junaina Abdullah, who helped in reviewing a set of videos on parenting, and to Layla Sein for her insightful comments.

Hasan Altalib, for providing the many enriching references and useful comments on the presentation, contents, and format of the text.

We have been fortunate to have Salwa Medani in our office who worked diligently on the manuscript and improved it on a daily basis. A great blessing descended on us in the person of Shiraz Khan in our London office. She is a very special and remarkable editor who is a goldmine of creativity and critical feedback and a wonderful source of encouragement.

We are deeply indebted to Dr. Imad-ad-Dean Ahmad, president of the Minaret of Freedom Foundation, for his meticulous editing, invaluable additions, and enriching suggestions.

We are extremely grateful to Sylvia Hunt for her rigorous copy-editing, to Salma Mirza for her extensive proofreading, and to Abdallateef Whiteman for his admirable design and layout. Special thanks also go to Hanna, Abdallateef's daughter, for her exquisite hand drawn illustrations. Our profound appreciation is extended to the staff of the IIIT London Office for the quality of their work and supervision of the production of the final version.

The invaluable suggestions and professional insight of the education and psychology experts, Dr. Ishaq Farhan, Dr. Abdul Latif Arabiyyat, Dr. Mahmoud Rashdan, Dr. Fathi Malkawi, and Dr. Abdul Rahman al Naqeeb who contributed significantly to the quality of the book.

We thank our families for providing a comforting and supportive environment to ease the pressures around us while we worked on the manuscript. Special appreciation goes to Dr. Ilham Altalib, Dr. Hisham's life partner for 46 years, without whose unlimited encouragement and sacrifice this work would not have seen the light of day. Her insights and invaluable comments on parenting were a continual source of inspiration in bringing the work to fruition. The bulk of time spent on this work was "borrowed" from family time together and in particular our grandchildren Yusif and Ameen, seven and five years old.

All praise goes to the All-Knowledgeable and All-Powerful, Who gave us the strength to accomplish the task.

Dedication

TO OUR BELOVED mothers and fathers, who flooded us with love, sacrifice, and compassion throughout our lives, cherishing our development and raising and nurturing us to the best of their ability. Although lacking in training and formal education, they emulated the practice of their parents before them, using wisdom, commonsense, and the verified experiences of past generations and civilizations, to teach us righteousness, faith, and self-reliance. May God shower His blessings upon their souls.

To all the parents on our planet today, struggling hard to raise successful children, who, though they mean well, yet need the necessary knowledge and skills to communicate wisely with their children, and create the happy loving family relationships and home environment we all so dearly desire.

To all the families who wish to raise their children to become men and women of caliber, possessing values and qualities of righteousness, honesty, courage, compassion, creativity, and faith, as well as strength of mind and a sense of responsible independence.

To our wives and children, who have endured much hardship and strain over the years, exuding endless patience and unfailing encouragement while we worked on the research and writing of this book.

To all of the above we dedicate this humble effort.

May the Compassionate Almighty, the One and Only, accept our sincere endeavors in trying to bring harmony, peace, and improvement to humankind.

Table of Contents

PARENT-CHILD RELATIONS: A GUIDE TO RAISING CHILDREN **viii**
AIMS AND OBJECTIVES **x**
INTRODUCTION **xii**

Sex and Sex Education: What Do We Tell Our Children?
• Introduction **2**
• What is Sex Education? **2**
• The American Scene **3**
• Perceptions of Mothers and Daughters in the USA **6**
• Values and Sex: Today and Yesterday **6**
• Why Sex Education? Should We Teach it? **8**
• What to Teach Children? **9**
• Sex Abuse! How Serious is it? **10**
• Abrahamic Traditions Forbid Fornication and Adultery **12**
• The Rationale Behind the Legal Punishment of Adultery and Fornication **13**
• Sexually Transmitted Diseases (STDs) **14**
• Boyfriend–Girlfriend Relations **15**
• Children Having Children: Abortion and Adoption in Islam **17**
    Abortion 18
    Adoption in Islam 19
• Homosexuality and Parents **20**
• Islamic Sex Education **23**
• Parents' Duty Towards Children **25**
• Sex and Hygiene: Menstruation, Pubic Hair, Circumcision, Seminal Fluid **26**
• Teenagers and Abstention **27**
• The Islamic Solution to the Sexual Dilemma: A Road Map for a Preventive Approach **29**
    Modesty (Ḥayā') 31
    Dress Code 35
    No Free Mixing and No Khalwah 35
    Peer Pressure and Other Factors 36
    What to Do 37
    Early Marriage 37
• The Dilemma of the Educational System vs. Early Marriage **39**
• Protecting Children from Sexual Abuse by Adults **41**
    Age Appropriate Children Be Made Aware About Prostitution 42
    When One's Child is a Victim of Incest or Rape 43
• A Curriculum for Islamic Sex Education **45**
• Activities 1–2 **47**

BIBLIOGRAPHY **49**

Parent-Child Relations: A Guide to Raising Children

SEX AND SEX EDUCATION: What Do We Tell Our Children? was originally published as a chapter in the book *Parent-Child Relations: A Guide to Raising Children*. This book has been written for all parents, whoever they are and wherever they may be. However, its concept is part of the long-term vision of the International Institute of Islamic Thought (IIIT) to arouse the Muslim world from the intellectual stagnation and decay into which it has fallen and to recapture the intellectual dynamism that once symbolized its great civilization. To promote its vision on parenting, the book focuses on the intellectual and moral regeneration of the Muslim mind and psyche through the medium of education. Although an examination of the methodology behind the intellectual demise of the Muslim world is not addressed in the book, Islamic Thought reform is the main theme promoted in IIIT publications and conferences to help revive Muslim intellectualism.

Practically, it is imperative that parents know how to raise good children since the psychological foundations of values and personality are largely developed at home in early childhood. *Parent-Child Relations* therefore focuses primarily on how cultural, educational, and social skills training in the home is the basis for the proper intellectual, psychological and emotional development of a child. Although the home is the source of the behavioral patterns influencing the child's thought processes in determining right from wrong, it is not enough simply to know what is right and to mechanically do it. Human will and emotion have to accept and desire what the mind considers to be right and to act accordingly; this is where the role of parents is pivotal. Schools and educational institutions teach historical data, facts, physical and technical skills, and provide information, which are to be complemented by the child's home and family life, for it is the latter that develops character, social skills and emotional strength.

Parent-Child Relations is meant to contribute to child development and upbringing and different forms of human leadership development. IIIT has organized many conferences and published key works to serve this purpose including: *A Training Guide for Islamic Workers* (translated into more than 20 languages), *Dalīl Maktabat al-Usrah al-Muslimah* (Guide to a Muslim Family Library), and *Azmat al-Irādah wa al-Wujdān al-Muslim* (Crisis in the Muslim Will and Psyche).

The idea to write a book on parent–child relations was suggested during a meeting of IIIT's Board of Trustees in August 1994 on Tioman Island, Malaysia. It was to be the third in a series of books to be published on human development and interpersonal communication by the Institute. Far earlier, and in response to a request by the IIIT, Dr. Isma'īl al Fārūqī authored in 1982 *Tawḥīd: Its Implications for Thought and Life* (a Muslim training manual on the issues of belief and *'aqīdah*). Later in 1991, the IIIT and the International Islamic Federation of Student Organizations (IIFSO) jointly published the widely successful *A Training Guide for Islamic Workers*, the second book in the series, which sought to educate Muslims in effective personal, group and leadership skills. *Parent-Child Relations:*

A Guide to Raising Children is to be considered the third book in the series.

Recognizing the importance of the family unit, Dr. AbdulHamid AbuSulayman, Rector of the International Islamic University, Malaysia (1988–1998), established a new mandatory course (culminating in a Diploma) on Family and Parenting with a view to disseminating the rationale and moral value of good parenting to students as well as to produce enough teachers to teach the course.

In addition, IIIT founders had initiated a series of leadership training seminars organized in three phases. The idea of producing a book on parenting was given precedence during phase 3:

Phase 1 (1975–1990) consisted of definition, preparation, propagation, and mobilization. It dealt with the skills and tools of activism needed to improve the efficiency and performance of work. This phase culminated in the publication of *A Training Guide for Islamic Workers* (1991), the second book in the series noted above.

Phase 2 (1991–2000) institutionalized training with the efforts of competent trainers including Dr. Omar Kasule in Kuala Lumpur, Dr. Iqbal Unus in Washington, Dr. Anas al-Shaikh-Ali in London and Dr. Manzoor Alam in New Delhi. They conducted numerous training programs worldwide.

Phase 3 was to focus on parenting in the twenty-first century. While Phases 1 and 2 targeted youth activists, it became increas-ingly clear that character building was an equally essential component that began at birth. As such, IIIT decided to emphasize the significant role that parents can play using good parenting skills to raise righteous citizens and future leaders imbued with principled leadership traits within a healthy and conducive home environment for children to grow. Hence, the publication of this work.

Parenting is not a job to be underestimated or taken lightly. It has a huge impact on the type of children we raise, the type of society in which we live, and ultimately the type of civilization we leave for future generations. As such, it should be given the utmost consideration and be made top priority. We cherish this belief deeply and strongly encourage and invite other authors to further develop each of the topics covered in this book with additional research and instructional materials. IIIT has already established several academic teams to develop further materials on these topics and has translated them into major world languages. *Parent-Child Relations: A Guide to Raising Children* is only the first step in promoting the case for proper parenting at the practical level.

According to many experts, "the largest trade in the world, the most important task, the greatest task, and the best investment of human beings is cherishing and raising children."

Aims and Objectives of Parent-Child Relations: A Guide to Raising Children

PARENT-CHILD RELATIONS: A GUIDE TO RAISING CHILDREN is an easy-to-read book which addresses the one billion parents of our world today, both Muslims and those of other faiths, as well as non-parents, grandparents and relatives who wish to benefit from its advice. It is not aimed at scholars and specialists in particular. Its specific focus is on the goals of parenting, highlighting problems and offering solutions, as well as outlining methods to develop and raise people of righteousness, moral caliber and who will demonstrate leadership qualities.

The main objectives of the work are to:

• Emphasize the importance of good parenting in raising children and families, by making parental responsibility a duty and a top priority, not just theoretically but practically.

• Show parents "how" to acquire the necessary education and skills to implement proper parenting techniques in order to raise righteous citizens of firm character and sound morals, who have the qualities needed to become the building blocks of society and future human civilization.

• Finally, to help parents to create a happy, harmonious and functional family home environment, with supportive relationships amongst all the family members.

Part One deals with the rationale behind good parenting, defining what it is and how it can be implemented to form a very real solution for the regeneration of the Muslim world as well as society as a whole. We also outline the status of parenting as practiced today, including reviewing sources of information available to the Muslim world and the world's industrialized countries, on parenting. We sought to examine how to raise children of sound moral character who possess qualities for active social change. The methods and tools needed to promote physical and emotional strength are highlighted in Part Two of the book. Part Three focuses on character-building and discusses the impact of too much television as well as computer and video games on children and family life while providing practical alternatives to their excessive use.

At the end of each chapter, the book includes user-friendly exercises to be performed by both parents and children. The main purpose is to promote ongoing dialog and communication among family members so they can come to know each other well, enjoy time together, participate in decision making, and exchange skills. This will help establish good dynamic family relationships and a happy home environment. Very few activities require outside resources like the use of a library, consulting other parents, or seeking professional advice. We strongly recommend that families do these activities at home or around dinner tables outside the home. It is hoped that these participatory and interactive discussions/activities will fill an important yet missing gap in daily parenting, facilitating discussions pertaining to internal family issues that are rarely tackled and usually marginalized. These discussions and family reflections are a worthwhile aim in themselves.

Finally, *Parent-Child Relations* and the issues it tackles will be followed by the publication of additional works on the subject, categorized under two major themes:

1: (a) Understanding the Role of Parents in Education, Faith, and Skills Training; (b) Happy Families: Necessary Incubators for Developing Future Potential Leaders.

In terms of 1(a) the idea is to help parents understand and accept their role in developing their children's concept of faith and leadership skills. In terms of 1(b) the focus will be on establishing a pleasant and comfortable family home environment to act as an "incubator" to nurture pious people who are potential leaders with a sense of civic responsibility. Issues of communication, praise, criticism, anger, and family time spent together represent the practical steps needed to build and provide the correct environment. In addition, the idea that "children are good observers, but poor analysts" will be illustrated. Practical tests will be provided for parents to see how children deal in real life with others, including with each other, grandparents and other relatives, guests, neighbors, the poor, the community, animals, plants, the environment and the world in general.

2: Role Models for Good Parenting are a Must: The Parents – the Prophets.

Parents will be made aware of the importance of their own behavior in relation to child development. Since children are imitators, parents must be the best role models they can be so that by emulating them children can be the best they can be.

The life of Prophet Muhammad ﷺ furnishes the best example of how to emulate being a father, a grandfather, a great friend of children and a great leader. Indeed, in studying the behavior of the Prophet ﷺ and using his conduct as a blueprint we will set the standard by which to apply the advice given in this entire work.

Finally, if parents do their best and succeed in implementing our suggestions, we hope to set in motion a positive cycle: the raising of healthy and happy children who are active participants in society and who themselves will eventually make exemplary parents.

If at some stage in life, mothers and fathers are ever asked: "What did you do to make your life worthwhile?" they can respond with confidence: "I was a great parent." Maybe a happy grandparent too!

Introduction

WHAT ARE CHILDREN BEING TAUGHT ABOUT SEX? What are they learning from peers, television, movies, magazines, computer games, pop music, popular culture etc.?

This publication has been produced to make it easy for parents to understand and broach the sensitive topic of sex education. It seeks to break the grip of mainstream popular culture and the entertainment industry, a key source of children's information, and to help parents tackle excessive and premature sexualisation. Originally forming chapter thirteen of *Parent-Child Relations: A Guide to Raising Children*, it charts a way forward.

Most parents are rightly alarmed by the increasingly controversial nature of the information being fed to children and how age-appropriate it actually is. Parents are also concerned that a sidelining of moral principles is taking place in favor of more and more sexually explicit content entering our homes and the daily landscape of our children's lives. For instance, what message is being conveyed to children, one of abstinence before marriage or safe sex using contraceptives? Of modesty or sex appeal?

Therefore, whilst parents may be uncomfortable talking to their children about sexuality they cannot afford not to and certainly ought not to rely on schools to absolve them of any responsibility in this regard. Even the vocabulary of sex is under threat with terminology being introduced unsuitable for the child/teenager and giving him/her a greater awareness of sexuality than appropriate. Although all is not cause for concern, for instance efforts to educate children on the dangers of STDs, HIV, Aids etc. are commendable, it is where the boundaries of propriety become confused with ethics that the moral message needs to be reinforced. And parents are ideally placed to do this.

Parents are not powerless. They can educate their children in a manner they feel appropriate and which maintains a sense of the sacred. This publication is designed to help them do this. The authors use a holistic approach to include what morality requires of humanity in this regard, and also focus on issues of healthy relationships, responsibility, emotional wellbeing, and good physical health. The publication is intended to give parents practical advice, using clear, precise information, to address some of the most common issues parents are likely to encounter and questions they are likely to face. The tone is reassuring and encouraging throughout.

One thing is certain, the subject itself cannot be ignored, for if we as parents do not teach our children right from wrong, weeding out negative elements and giving them a sound understanding of sex based on core values and respect, we will be leaving them open to interpretations which come right off the pages of glossy magazines, big hit movies and everywhere else they turn in society, exposing them to marketing that teaches men to view women as objects, and women to look like fashion models.

IIIT London Office
January 2014

Sex and Sex Education: What Do We Tell Our Children?

Introduction

Sex and sex education are topics of immense importance and profound significance. Most parents feel extremely uncomfortable when discussing sex, preferring to leave the sex education of their children to schools and other people. For people to be physically fit and healthy, in mind, body, heart, and soul, they have to deal properly with sex. The unlawful practice of sex leads to tragedy, and long-term damage. The best known of these are social and physical diseases. It is not just the individuals participating in unlawful sex who can be infected with diseases, but their spouses and offspring may be harmed as well. The damage can be so severe that it becomes incurable.

Our Maker, the Creator, prohibited fornication and adultery (*zinā*). Sexual promiscuity brings disaster, so one of the foremost rules is that sex must be confined to marriage. Sexually transmitted diseases (STDs) arise from engaging in unlawful sex. When the human race behaves in an unnatural way, new kinds of diseases may strike. Parents need to take an active part in sex education for themselves and for their children.

What is Sex Education?

PEOPLE HAVE DIFFERENT perceptions of sex education. Is it about the anatomy and physiology of the human body, or sexual intercourse, or reproduction and family life, or the prevention of disease and unwanted pregnancies? Is educating children about sex equivalent to giving them permission to engage in sex? A teacher once said: "I am not planning to tell your children whether or not they should engage in sex, or how to do it. But in case they do decide to do it, they should know how to prevent disease and pregnancy." Most sex education programs are incomplete and avoid issues of morality, sexual dysfunction, deviation, and marriage.

There are two basic issues. One consists of biological facts. These deal with teenage fears that arise when youngsters have not been prepared by their parents about menstruation or nocturnal emissions. Another basic issue is giving sexually active young people enough information to avoid unwanted pregnancies and any consequent abortions. Information helps to safeguard them from danger.

Some schools teach the simple mechanics of physical reproduction as well as moral responsibility. Other schools provide bits and pieces of information. In many schools, sex education is a large part of the *Moral and Social Education* curriculum. It does little good to remove your child from these classes, for the subjects discussed may also arise in English or History, or Physical Education, or Art, or the weekly Religious Education program, or virtually anywhere else. Sex has become an integral part of our life.

Most sex education does not encourage a happy and fulfilled married life. Thus, many spouses have very frustrating married lives, frequently owing to the lack of knowledge and skills. The common misconception is that "the man's ability to arouse or satisfy his wife will just come naturally." Knowledge of how to create a happy marriage is a crucial part of education. What a pity that this education is not provided somewhere in the youngster's life.

If your teenager has become sexually active, you will probably be the last person to know about it. The teenager would obviously try to keep it secret. Moreover, teenagers have a secretive network among themselves, where they know a lot about their peers, and vice versa, but all is concealed from the parents.

The real satisfactory answer is the model of the Prophet ﷺ. The way sex education is defined and taught in schools has many positives and negatives. Hence, parents have to shoulder the responsibility of guiding their children. The sex information we are given by society, including schools, TV, the Internet, and peers, has mixed advantages and disadvantages.

The American Scene

Athar (1990) relates how children are being given value-free sex education in school as well as the wrong message from the media. (See *Sex Education: An Islamic Perspective,* edited by Shahid Athar, M.D. http://www. teachislam.com/dmdocuments/33/BOOK/ SexEducation). In most schools, sex education is taught from grades 2 to 12, at a cost of billions of dollars. Teachers describe the technical aspects of sex without telling children about moral values or how to make the right decisions. After describing the anatomy and physiology of reproduction, the main emphasis is on the prevention of venereal diseases and teenage pregnancy. With the rise of AIDS,

the focus is on "safe sex," which normally means using condoms. Tax dollars are paid to some schools for dispensing free condoms and other contraceptives to those who go to school health clinics. Condom vending machines are available in some school hallways and in universities.

The role of parents is minimized and sometimes ridiculed. Whenever young boys ask a question about sex, their fathers usually shun them and change the subject. Therefore, the boys learn about sex from strangers. Some vices promoted by educators are unacceptable according to religious principles. According to Dr. Shahid Athar, the beliefs of some misguided educators are as follows:

(a) Nudity in homes (in the shower or bedroom) is good and a healthy way to introduce sexuality to smaller (under 5) children, giving them an opportunity to ask questions. Yet according to a 1997 study 75% of all child molestations and incests (500,000 per year) occur by a close relative (parent, step parent or another family member) in a familiar surrounding. (Abel et al. 2001)

(b) A child's playing with the genitals of another child is a "naive exploration", is permissible and is not a reason for either scolding or punishment. This particular educator is also aware that boys as young as 12 have raped girls as young as 8. He does not inform us

when this "naive exploration" becomes a sex act.

(c) Children caught reading 'dirty' magazines should not be made to feel guilty, but parents should use this as a chance to get some useful points across to him or her about sexual attitudes, values and sex exploitation. This is astonishing ignorance. Many of these magazines convey the message that sex is a commodity and that women are toys for men to play with. In fact, guilt is not a harmful emotion as long as it gets people to regret an action and to correct it. Feeling remorse through guilt (in order to evaluate and reverse a wrong act) is a learning mechanism for teaching children to measure their behavior and feel responsibility.

(d) If one's child is already sexually active, instead of telling them to stop it, the parents' moral duty is to protect their health and career by providing them information and means for contraception and avoiding venereal disease. Educators such as these do not believe that giving sexual information means giving the go ahead signal for sex. Yet, if someone is told the shape, color, smell and taste of a new fruit, and the pleasure derived from eating it, doesn't common sense dictate

True or False?

The More They Know it, the More They do it!!

that they would like to try it? Parents need to initiate appropriate discussion concerning improper sexual relations. The discussion can be about a community member's unwanted pregnancy, a vulgar advertisement, lewd music or a TV show that promotes promiscuity.

Sex education in American public schools has not decreased the incidence of teenage venereal disease or teenage pregnancy nor has it changed the sexual habits of teenagers. Unfortunately, going to church is not helping much either. (Athar 1990)

Unless your children go to a school that actually tries to prevent biological knowledge, they are going to experience some sex education, and parents should be more involved. Schools usually give simple biological knowledge and contraception information needed by youngsters

who are becoming adults. Many Muslim parents, like those of other faiths, are concerned that the sexual morals imparted in government schools are not up to the standards of their faith, and that to give children advice on contraception may encourage them to have sex. This is a false fear, for the information given is factual and necessary to the young person.

Many men, Muslim and non-Muslims, are surprised to discover the sexual hunger of their wives. This is because many men have been told that it is easy for a woman to satisfy a man's sexual needs, for all she has to do is to keep still and give him access for a few seconds. However, men have not been told that it is a matter of skill and a religious duty for a man to learn to satisfy a woman's sexual needs. They have to overcome their natural shyness about a woman's private parts, to learn foreplay techniques, and grasp the understanding that if they satisfy themselves and leave the woman "hungry," they are causing severe deprivation to their wives and this is a form of cruelty.

Most parents do not want their children to start indiscriminately "sleeping around". Nevertheless, once their teenager begins to have a private life away from their watchful eye, the parents will have very little control. Although innocence is one way of protecting youngsters, the kind of innocence desired by parents has usually disappeared in the playground before the child is 10 years old. Children these days take in knowledge from the Internet, television and movies, and if your children have access to DVDs (or friends with DVDs), the sexual "knowledge" gained from what they watch is likely to be far "in advance" of your own, realistically speaking.

AIDS One of Leading Causes of Death in Thailand

AIDS in 2001 became the leading cause of death in Thailand, overtaking accidents, heart disease and cancer, according to Deputy Public Health Minister Surapong Suebwong-lee. The minister did not disclose exact figures but said the extent of HIV-AIDS had been under-reported because the relatives of victims in rural areas were reluctant to report the real cause of death.

"Village headmen reported most non-accidental deaths as being a result of 'the heart stopped beating'. This led to a misconception that most Thais die of heart disease". "But we have done a new random survey and found out that the biggest cause of deaths in the rural areas is AIDS," he said after returning from a World Health Organisation meeting in the Maldives. The UN Programme on HIV-AIDS (UNAIDS) office in Bangkok stated that AIDS deaths would continue to rise as Thais who were infected at the start of the epidemic 10 years ago have begun to sicken and die in large numbers. An estimated one million of Thailand's 60 million people have been infected with HIV and around one third of those have already died. (AIDS EDUCATION GLOBAL INFORMATION SYSTEM 2001)

Why Did an Otherwise Content Professor Choose to Leave the USA?

A professor at the International Islamic University, Malaysia (IIUM) once related the following story. His third-grade son in a government elementary school in Michigan had come home one day and explained in great detail a classmate's performance of the full sexual act in the classroom with a schoolgirl! This caused the professor to pack up and leave America with his family of five children! The result of value-neutral sex education has produced a generation indulging in sex in a casual, irresponsible way. The prevalent culture has made sex attractive, available, enjoyable, and accessible. Avoidance seems abnormal to many, because sexual images and promiscuity have become common.

Perceptions of Mothers and Daughters in the USA

Teenagers are growing more confused about sexual behavior, and they are lacking the appropriate guidance from parents and teachers. Below are some examples of what teenagers are saying:

- Says 16-year-old Selma: "I can't ask my mother anything about sex. If I do, she starts wondering why I asked the question. 'What do you want to know for?' she insists, 'unless…'"
- Says 14-year-old Juliet: "My mother believes that ignorance assures innocence. She gets mad when I ask her anything about sex. She says, 'Your husband will teach you all you need to know about sex.'"
- Says 18-year-old Louis: "I get a mixed message from my parents. One says, 'Don't do it, you'll get into trouble!' The other says, 'Sow your wild oats while you are young.' I wish parents would make up their minds. If sex is good for us, let them say so. If it is bad for us, then don't tempt, don't provoke, and don't confuse."
- Says 15-year-old Joshua: "My father always wants us to be truthful. But his honesty stops where sex begins. This is one area where my candor is not welcomed."
- 22-year-old Jonathan says: "For college boys, sex is a symbol of maturity and masculinity. For girls, it's a safeguard against unpopularity and loneliness."
- The dilemma of sex is expressed by a teenager: "If I see a comedy, I can laugh; a tragedy, I can cry; something that makes me angry, I can scream; but if I see a play that has me sexually aroused, what can I do then?"

These discussions indicate that appropriate sex education is now needed to serve as an antidote to ignorance. Society can no longer passively permit the street and the screen to set its sex standards and values.

Values and Sex: Today and Yesterday

There is a considerable conflict of values among people today. Some parents feel that the time has come to accept the new reality. They are worried about STDs, unwanted pregnancies, and ruined reputations. They hope to avoid these dangers with candid sex education. Some would supply their teenagers with information and contraception.

Other parents indignantly reject these measures. They know that contraceptives might encourage pre-marital sex. They know that society cannot support teenage sex because early erotic awakening would endanger responsible human relationships and civilization. The main task of youth is to acquire knowledge and prepare themselves for a righteous adult and family life. To accomplish this task it is best to keep the "lid on the id." Some find even discussion of sex repugnant and in bad taste. Some parents feel that open sex talk will stimulate sex acts, even when the goal is self-control. One parent talks of being role models to children: "Only when we adults set a decent example and demand decent behavior will children become the kind of people we like."

Both in life and literature, there is less sexual morality. In the United States and many other countries sex is no longer a forbidden subject; it is taught in school and discussed at home.

In these societies it is taken for granted that if exposed to temptation, youth will give in.

Therefore, boys are suspected and girls are chaperoned. Boys nowadays have cars and many girls have freedom. When maximum temptation exists with minimum supervision, how can we realistically expect youth to follow the moral rules?

In the past, nice girls insisted on chastity and when confronted with an insistent boyfriend, allowed necking or petting only. This was her compromise with conscience and society. Now, many teenagers are pushed to question this solution. Boys resent it because TV, movies and magazines leave them over-stimulated, and girls resent it because it turns them into teasers.

College girls in these countries who want to stay virgins find it hard. Many boys refuse to date them and some girls treat them as old fashioned. Those who are serious about "saving themselves for marriage" may find themselves socially isolated. Under these pressures, a virgin may start doubting her normality. In the face of temptation and ridicule, only the morally determined can maintain their high standards. Sadly, many girls have sex in this environment, not out of need but out of pressure. In the past, a girl could use the fear of pregnancy as an excuse for chastity. Now this excuse is gone. Prophylactics are sold at supermarkets, pills and diaphragms are easily obtained, and some schools and even churches distribute free condoms.

During a visit from college, Jason, aged 18, said to his father about life and love: "I have discovered the real difference between boys and girls. Girls play with sex as a way of getting love. Boys play with love as a means of getting sex. My philosophy is love them and leave them." His father asked, "What happens to the girl after you and other guys love her and leave her?" "It is not my business, I try not to think about it," said Jason.

"Well, think about it. In the Orient, they say if you save a man from death, you are responsible for his life. If you devised a strategy to lure a girl into love, her feelings become your business," answered his father.

Jason's father affirmed a basic principle: Honesty and responsibility pertain to all human relations. All situations, simple or complex, social or sexual, require individual integrity and accountability.

Why Sex Education? Should We Teach it?

Teenagers are eager to learn all they can about sex. They are troubled and perplexed and demand realistic and personal answers. When offered an opportunity to discuss sex seriously, teenagers talk freely and sensibly. They look for standards and meaning, wanting to come to terms with their sexuality.

The question is: should sex education be offered to teenagers? Often, this comes too late. Sex is already being poorly taught on the internet, in the schoolyard, and in the streets. In words and pictures, children are being exposed to sex that is often sordid and vulgar. The screens and the streets are a ceaseless source of misinformation. Smut-sellers never hesitate to share sex "facts" and feelings. Precocious peers willingly tell of experiences, real and imagined. It is the parents and teachers who often fear to share the proper information in a timely manner.

Sex education has two parts: information and values. Values are best learned at home. Experts can best give information. Not all questions on sex spring from a thirst for knowledge. Some children aim to embarrass their parents, who need not answer provocative questions. Parents cannot be expected to be candid, comfortable, and knowledgeable about every aspect of human sexuality. Information sought genuinely should be provided, whereas other questions are best referred to experts. Parents need to encourage their teenagers to take part in discussions on sex sponsored not only by the school, but more importantly by the church, mosque, and the community center. Information imparted objectively and honestly can decrease hostility

and increase trust between the generations. Adults may regain their faith in youth, and young people may find that despite the age gap, adults really are concerned with their well-being and share with them a common humanity.

On the other hand, one may argue: Do children need sex education? Do you teach a baby duck how to swim or just put it in water and let it swim? For thousands of years men and women have had sex without formal education. In many traditional civilizations, sex education starts by trial and error after marriage. However, having a dozen children is not a proof of love. An appropriate and healthy sex

education is crucial to the fulfillment of a happy marriage.

Who should teach sex education? Everyone has a role to play. The parents need to know the facts and the issues of concern and have to assume a more responsible role. The father has a duty to be able to answer his son's questions, and the mother, her daughter's questions. We cannot rely on sex education at school or from the media. It is our duty to supplement it with an ethical and moral dimension. Sunday school teachers, the family physician, the pediatrician, well-informed imams, and the clergy can also play a role. Within a family, the older sister has a duty toward the younger one and the elder brother toward the younger one.

Parents should not be silent about sex education. Silence sends the wrong message to children. Children are confused by the conflicting "facts" they hear from strangers and peers. They will develop undesirable attitudes about sexuality which could affect them negatively during their adult years.

Avoiding sex education is not an option any more. We must be realistic. Parents who try to prevent their children from having sex education are really banging their heads against a brick wall. It is surely better for their children to learn from a learned and ethically responsible adult, who will be able to undo any possible confusion and undesirable influences of the environment.

The Qur'an and the Prophet ﷺ discuss sex issues clearly and wisely. Sex is not a dirty word, for it is an important aspect of human lives. The Qur'an discusses in a dignified language: reproduction, creation, family life, menstruation, and ejaculation. The Prophet ﷺ discussed respectfully with his Companions many aspects of their sexual lives in this regard. One reason why Muslim parents do not discuss sex is due to the way in which they have been brought up. Parents may be ignorant about sex, or uncomfortable with their own sexuality or its expression.

What to Teach Children?

Many parents prepare their daughters for the onset of monthly periods, and their sons for their first nocturnal emission. Some parents do not prepare their kids, which causes fear and distress to the teenager. Any unexpected discharge or blood is automatically connected in the young person's mind with a disease or damage, and if it has followed any self-exploration or masturbation, the young person can feel worried and guilty. A heavy flow of blood or semen often makes them believe that

something inside them has broken or is diseased, and they are too ashamed and frightened to talk about it. One young girl was desperately trying to cope with her bleeding with handkerchiefs for months, thinking she was seriously ill, and too frightened to tell anybody. At last, a kind teacher discovered her bloodstained clothes and helped her. She had been desperately washing them out in case her mother saw them.

Some mothers need to think about their own wrong attitudes toward menstruation before they talk to their daughters about it. It is useful if boys know something about it too. It helps later, when a young man has to cope with a wife who is suffering from pain, premenstrual tension, or a bad temper. It is quite pointless to regard the whole business as unclean and embarrassing, and treat the girl during this time as a person to be shunned.

The Prophet ﷺ advised that we should not hurt menstruating women by rejecting them or making them feel unclean. Only full sexual intercourse should be avoided. However, so long as the woman's private parts were covered and the man protected from blood, the couple could find satisfaction how they liked.

With few exceptions, sex education in the American public secondary schools has mostly become a series of lessons on how to use condoms, avoid diseases, and obtain abortions. The prevailing attitude in the United States seems to be that young people are going to have sex anyway, so we should just help them to do it safely. A moral or ethical perspective is rarely given, and if it is, there are no references to religion, spirituality, and pleasing God. Mixed-sex classes remove a young person's natural sense of shyness. Even in single-sex classes children are encouraged to experiment with sex, and given tips on kissing techniques or masturbation as part of a "natural exploration of sexuality." Muslim children who have not had any previous exposure to these topics will not know how to respond, and may be too embarrassed to ask their parents about it.

Sex Abuse! How Serious is it?

According to Islam, any sexual intercourse outside marriage (*zinā*) is a form of moral and religious abuse. Some argue that when sex abuse results in illegitimate children, it may be more devastating – in some cases – to a society than murder. Adultery can have a very long-term effect on families and society for generations to come. The outcome of adultery may be manifested in one or more of the following ways: diseases, abortion, handicapped or retarded babies (if an STD – sexually transmitted disease – is passed to a pregnant wife), illegitimate children, single-parent families, broken families, confused lineage (*nasab*), betrayal of trust, and prostitution.

Adultery cheapens human dignity and interaction. A society that allows for the violation of sexual taboos (such as adultery) may end up with more serious sexual taboos (such as prostitution) regardless of whether it is illegal. Once taboos are violated on a small scale, they become easier to violate on a larger scale. Fornication and adultery are major sins punishable by the Almighty in this life and in the Hereafter.

Islam does not regard fornication and adultery as personal sins only, but rather as aggressions against society. If they become acceptable, they destroy the fabric of society, starting from its very foundation, the family. Indeed, the legal punishment for fornication and adultery in the Qur'an is a public lashing of one hundred stripes. So severe is the danger of adultery to society that in the ancient past, stoning was required (i.e. The Bible,

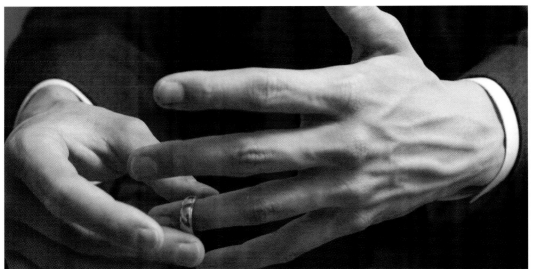

Deut. 22:23–24). Stoning however is not prescribed in the Qur'an and many Muslim scholars reject the validity of stoning outright. Owing to the seriousness and dishonor associated with the charge of adultery, four sane, reliable, adult Muslim witnesses must testify to the court the details of the act of adultery. The requirement of the four witnesses is both to protect the privacy and honor of the suspects and also to convey the message that fornication and adultery are social concerns as well. All people are innocent unless four credible witnesses testify to the contrary. Fewer than four reliable witnesses is not valid evidence and jurists may agree that DNA tests can be accepted as evidence. Adultery committed in front of four or more witnesses is a public propagation of evil in the society rather than just a personal lust satisfaction through secret means.

Adultery is, in addition, a violation of the marital contract. About half of all first-time marriages in the United States result in divorce within two years and the main reason is an extramarital affair by either spouse. Many people are not heeding either the Bible or the Qur'an. The Bible states, "Thou shalt not commit adultery," and the Qur'an resonates: "Do not approach adultery," which means that not only is it illegal, but also that we should avoid anything that leads to it. All approaches to adultery (such as dating, provocative clothing, nudity, obscenity, and pornography) are included in the condemnation. The dress codes for men and women are ordained to protect both from temptation and lust by onlookers. Some men lose self-control and fall into a major sin and possibly rape!

In matters of sex, attitudes speak louder than words. What is the society's true attitude toward sex? What is our concept of morality? As a society, we lack role models of moral excellence. Thoughtful teenagers are puzzled by a prevalent public paradox: on the one hand, society is sex-obsessed and money-motivated. For fun and profit, sex is portrayed in movies, blown up on billboards, and used for commercial enticement. On the other hand, society declares that it believes in *premarital abstinence*. This situation creates conflict and tension. If society permits continual public sources of stimulation, it cannot prevent private sources of abuse and relief. Many young people have "liberated" ideas that "being in love" consists in having sex with anyone, regardless of their lack of commitment. This leads to sexual encounters, and also divorce.

Natalie, a 19 year-old college sophomore, explains her dilemma
(Faber and Mazlish 1982):

> My parents and I live by the grace of unspoken code: No deep questions, no real an-
> swers. They really don't want to know what goes on. And I can't tell them. I am a good
> girl with conventional morals. To start with, it is hard for me to find a fellow who
> would love me in a friendly way. I like to date. The first few meetings are pleasant.
> Then comes the pressure: you are invited to parties with liquor and marijuana. It is
> taken for granted that you will go to bed with him. And they say, "If you do, the world
> will smile with you. If you don't, you'll cry alone." So I'm full of integrity and tears.

The disastrous result is that some children cannot tell right from wrong. The United
States has an AIDS problem, a drug problem, and a violence problem. None of these problems will go away until schools once again make it their job to teach good character. The
school curriculum must create a moral environment that complements parental guidance.
Schools that are courageous enough to reinforce and practice virtue are better at building
a healthy society than an army of doctors, counselors, police, and social workers.

Abrahamic Traditions Forbid Fornication and Adultery

The following sequence, totally or partially, is common in today's young
generation:

Boyfriend–Girlfriend → Temptation and Seduction → Premarital intercourse → Loss of virginity and honor → unwanted pregnancy →(abortion or forced early marriage or illegitimate children followed by
adoption) → poverty and misery → breaking of family ties → diseases
→ death!

A person who is sexually promiscuous may
contract gonorrhea, syphilis, herpes, or AIDS,
and then pass these disease(s) on to an innocent spouse. If the wife happens to be
pregnant, the disease may harm their child
permanently. The baby could be born blind
or handicapped. If AIDS is contracted, the
man is responsible for the slow, painful
death of his wife and child, as well as himself!

Adultery causes havoc when children are

involved. A man may father children from
other women and refuse to take responsibility
for those children since he is not legally married
to their mother(s). By his deceitful actions, he
denies his children the right to be brought up
in a secure, dignified, and stable home. Likewise,
a woman who has sex with someone other
than her husband may become pregnant with
another man's child. If she hides this fact from
everyone, she cannot hide it from her own

conscience. Also the child may never know his/her real father and other relatives. The real father will not be able to act as a father to his child, and the woman's husband is cheated and will unwittingly be responsible for a child who is not his own. By her deceitful actions, she takes away the basic right of everyone to know his/her real family. The cheated father and/or the child may discover the truth by blood-matching or a DNA test. She may also catch and spread diseases such as AIDS, threatening the lives of her husband and children. Normally, a married person who has an extra-marital affair is discovered sooner or later, and this often leads to disaster and divorce, which has serious effects on the children, the family, and society.

In Islam, the punishments for adultery can be applied only in a court that officially applies Islamic law. Individuals cannot and must not take the law into their own hands, but should go to the authority with the required evidence. Unfortunately, some fathers have lost their tempers and murdered their daughters – along with their boyfriends – who have become pregnant before marriage out of their "sense of honor." Some of these "murders" (honor killings) are based on mere suspicion of misconduct, and the boyfriends, having greater freedom of movement, usually escape.

There is so much social pressure for teenagers to fit in and listen to their peers and the media. If they would instead listen to their conscience, these problems could be avoided. Unmarried people who try out sex before marriage discover (although too late) that it was just not worth it. In exchange for a few minutes of fun, they find themselves facing a lifetime of trouble and sadness. This might have been the worst decision they have ever taken in their lives. And on the Day of Judgment, they will have to answer to the Almighty for their actions.

The Rationale Behind the Legal Punishment of Adultery and Fornication

Although it seems strange to modern ears to consider fornication and adultery a crime, yet within Islam it is just this, illustrating the great extent to which these actions inflict harm on human lives and society. The subject requires a deep understanding of the nature of human beings. We will look at four elements: the Divine Revelation, reason, nature, and the action itself.

The main aim of the law of punishment is to establish peace and security in the society. When the crime is related to material wealth or homicide, Islamic law requires only two witnesses to establish the facts. However, if the crime is related to adultery (lust and desire), four witnesses are needed. Why? Because the issue here is not just the committing of the sin individually, but also the effect of its public commission on society, that is, in the presence of at least four people. Public commission of this sin is an avenue to spreading evil and vice.

There is also the need to balance the suppression of vice and the protection of privacy and honor. There is a considerable difference between sinning in secret to satisfy a human desire and sinning publicly to spread vice among people and threaten their honor and security. A good example is that of the second caliph, 'Umar ibn al-Khaṭṭāb, who – when passing by a house – heard people singing and drinking and climbed the wall of the house to investigate. Although he wanted to prosecute them, they countered that the Caliph had no right to climb the wall and spy on them. He realized his mistake and did not take any action against them. In the case of adultery, if there are fewer than four witnesses, then they should never utter a word about what they have witnessed, otherwise they will be punished for libel and scandal in society. Islam discourages promoting sins and vices because it makes them more familiar, allowing for their gradual acceptance and toleration by society.

Sexually Transmitted Diseases (STDs)

Teenagers can contract a disease called "mono" (mononucleosis) just from kissing each other; it attacks the liver and requires several weeks of bed-rest. Other contagious diseases that are spread through sexual contact are:

- gonorrhea, which can make men and women sterile (unable to have children)
- genital herpes, which causes very painful blisters on one's genitalia and recurs repeatedly throughout a person's life
- syphilis, which can damage almost every part of the human body
- AIDS (Auto Immune Deficiency Syndrome) which leads to a slow and painful death. Treatment with antiretroviral drugs can delay the onset of AIDS for several decades.

Faithful married couples that do not have sexual intercourse with anyone except each other do not contract venereal diseases. STDs are spread either by unmarried people who have several partners, or by married people who are unfaithful to their spouses and secretly have sex with others. In the 1940's, the well known sexually transmitted diseases were syphilis and gonorrhea. Now new ones are identified every few years and are becoming increasingly harder to treat. For AIDS and herpes, there is no known cure.

In a way, these diseases are a deterrent to prevent deviation from a pure nature as a result of publicly sinful societies.

> **The Prophet ﷺ said:**
>
> "Whenever sexual deviation becomes spread in a society and publicly acceptable, then plague and other diseases which were not previously known to their predecessors will appear and spread among them."
>
> (IBN MĀJAH)

The health hazards of pre-marital sex also include sexual trauma, cervical cancer, and unwanted teenage pregnancy.

A variety of injuries are possible when the sexual organs are not sufficiently mature for sex. Some of these injuries have a long-lasting effect. Cervical cancer is thought to be related to sex occurring at an early age with multiple partners.

The sexual revolution in the 1960's in the United States increased the costs of health care. In 1985 alone, ten million cases of chlamydia, two million cases of gonorrhea, one million cases of venereal warts, half a million cases of genital herpes and 90,000 cases of syphilis were diagnosed. The plague of AIDS is adding to our fears.

> **Risk factors for cervical cancer include: Multiple sex partners and smoking. Women at an increased risk ought to be getting regular Pap tests. (Cancer Research UK)**
>
> **The US has the highest rate of curable STDs of any developed country. More than 12 million people, including three million teens, become infected annually. (Institute of Medicine 1997)**

Boyfriend–Girlfriend Relations

Very young children do not mind with whom they play, although from about the age of eight, most boys prefer to play with boys and most girls prefer to play with girls. Children often form "best friend" relationships between the ages of 10 and 12, and keep these close friendships throughout their teens (D'Oyen 1996). When a man grows up, his friendships with other men continue to be important. If all is well in the family, he has a close relationship with his father, brothers, uncles, and cousins, and later on, his grown-up sons. A married woman continues to find great comfort in her friendship with other women like her mother and sisters, relatives, neighbors, or other women.

Innocent friendships are fine as long as they are kept within certain limits. A boy and a girl who are not closely related or *maḥram* (persons who are not allowed to marry each other) must not spend time alone together in a private place; they should both be modest and shy in their dress and behavior, and restrict their conversation to polite topics. Dating and intimate boy–girl friendships, which are prevalent in many societies, are not permitted in Islam. Family get-togethers, activities at the mosque, and friendly visits can provide plenty of opportunities for exchanging ideas and having a good time between boys and girls within the limits of modesty.

In many societies, it is common for boys and girls to go out together on dates and have several boyfriends and girlfriends before they finally marry. They mistakenly believe they will have a better chance of having a good marriage if they practice sex before marriage. Or they think they must try out different partners before they find the right one. Or they just want to "have fun." Sometimes they live together as husband and wife without getting married; this is called "living together." They might even have a child before they decide to get married, or they might decide never to get married.

This behavior is forbidden by many religions because of the terrible problems it causes. Sadly, the pressure on young people to behave in this way is becoming stronger. Television commercials, films, the Internet, and books at school are constantly trying to convince people that if they do not have a boyfriend or girlfriend, there is something wrong with them! Some schoolchildren as young as nine try to act much older by boasting about the things they have done with the other sex, as though they lead very exciting lives. They try to make other children feel that they are old-fashioned or stupid if they do not join them. But what really happens to these children as they get older?

Young people who are actively involved with the opposite sex at a very early age often come from problem families. Their parents may be divorced, or they may lack love or attention at home. They look for friendships with people of the opposite sex, who will kiss and touch them and keep them company. This is dangerous, because their feelings can easily get out of hand and lead to sexual intercourse before they are ready for it, and this will multiply their problems.

When teenagers have boyfriends or girlfriends before marriage, in the eyes of a Muslim, they become "used" like second-hand clothing. If they go so far as to have sexual intercourse before marriage, they lose their virginity. Many traditional cultures around the world emphasize virginity (for girls in particular) at marriage, and those girls who behave in a careless way lose their honor and have difficulty finding respectable husbands. However, Islam places a high and equal value on the self-control and chastity of both men and women. Most parents in these cultures will refuse to marry their daughter to a young man who is

known to be promiscuous and has had girl-friends. Such a man may grow tired of his wife before long and leave her for another woman, or he may not respect and treat her well.

Sexual intercourse can result in pregnancy because birth control is not always effective. If a girl becomes pregnant from fornication, it is a disaster for her and her baby and a disgrace for her family. Motherhood is an awesome responsibility even for a mature woman within a functioning family. It becomes unmanageable for a girl who becomes an unwed mother at the age of 11 to a child whose 14-year-old father is not prepared for fatherhood, and who are both thrust into these positions without the support of their families. It is less likely that they have matured educationally, emotionally, and economically. Therefore, they cannot provide a good life for themselves and their child. This is unfair to the innocent baby. More often, the boy becomes terrified and refuses to admit that he is the father of the child, and will not have anything to do with the girl after that. Then she is completely alone with a baby who will miss the love and support of a father. Such

people have a very difficult time. They may not be able to finish their studies, and both parents may have to take on unpleasant work to pay the bills.

In liberal societies, what can parents do about their daughter and the obsession of girls with boys? As their daughter grows, the parents may notice that she is noticing boys. They will hear her talking about that "hot" boy over there. The first time the parents hear her talking about an illicit relationship, they might feel a little nervous. Thoughts of such a boy (who they consider a monster) taking a liking to their daughter, then attempting to form a physical relationship with her will make the parents feel nauseated.

It is important that the daughter's heart is filled with a father's love and she is taught self-respect, responsibility, and values, so that when she encounters a man with less nobility and virtue (and more active hormones), she will not be vulnerable to his pressure. Since her parents have taught her how to talk to them, she will tell them about boys. When the secrecy is gone, the parents' fear will subside.

Teaching her the art of conversation will also protect her physically from boys, for she will have the confidence and skill to say, "that's unacceptable," rather than quietly acquiesce to his requests.

Parents should explain to their daughter the myths of falling in love with boys. Many times boys try to trick girls, and some girls try to trick boys! A "good" girl can justify her passion for sex by falling in love. This is one reason why a teenage girl is so vulnerable to romance and to "sweet" words by boys. Words of love may justify to her the act of love. She assumes that what is true for her is also true for boys. A boy is physically and psychologically different, and is brought up differently. A boy can make love without loving, and often finds himself sexually excited, even in the absence of girls. He may then look for relief, and "She" can be almost anyone. The double standard permits him to make love without involvement. "Have a good time, but don't bring her home," is the misleading advice for boys.

It is a girl's task not to allow herself to be used as a tool, and it is a boy's obligation not to use a girl as a tool. Both boys and girls need to know that there are strict rules for love and sex. It is unfair of a girl to tease and provoke a boy. It is unfair for a boy to pressure a girl. A boy may follow his misguided lust blindly and may go as far as the girl will let him, without questioning her readiness or his responsibility.

Children Having Children: Abortion and Adoption in Islam

Premarital intercourse is a form of sex abuse that could result in pregnancy. In spite of all the contraception used by teenagers, a considerable number of unwanted pregnancies occur among unwed mothers. It is devastating for the unwed pregnant teenager. On top of the psychological trauma, she must decide between two evils: abortion or becoming an unwed mother with an illegitimate baby forever. Such cases are not rare: one million unwed teenage girls become pregnant in the United States every year.

FINALLY, HE ADMITTED …

WHILST STUDYING AT LIVERPOOL UNIVERSITY IN THE UK BACK IN 1962, I HAPPENED TO HAVE A MUSLIM FRIEND WHO WOULD REGULARLY DATE THE LOCAL NON-MUSLIM GIRLS. I WOULD ARGUE ABOUT THE ILLS OF DATING, BUT IN VAIN. AFTER THREE YEARS OF CONTINUAL DATING HOWEVER, HE ONCE TOLD ME "YOU KNOW, YOU WILL BE HAPPY WHEN YOU MARRY BECAUSE BOTH YOU AND YOUR WIFE WILL BE VIRGINS ON YOUR WEDDING DAY SO IT WILL BE THE FIRST INTIMATE RELATIONSHIP THAT YOU EXPERIENCE, AND THE GIFT OF THIS WILL BE PRECIOUS AND FULFILLING. AS FOR ME, WHEN I MARRY MY WIFE WILL BE JUST ANOTHER OF THE MANY GIRLS I SLEPT WITH. SO FOR ME THE INTIMACY WILL NEITHER BE A SPECIAL NOR A DIGNIFIED ONE!"

What is life like for American teenagers who experience a pregnancy? Only 50 percent complete high school. More than 50 percent of them are dependent on welfare. They are more likely to become child abusers and their grown-up children have an 82 percent incidence of teenage pregnancy. Billions of dollars are spent every year on the financial and healthcare support of these teenage mothers in the United States.

There are No Illegitimate Children Only Illegitimate Parents with Innocent Babies!!

(WEISS 2007)

ABORTION

It is too late: parents have discovered that their daughter is pregnant. What can they do – as parents – to resolve the situation? Wisdom dictates that a DNA test be taken to identify the father of the baby. He should then be required to marry the "bachelorette" and make an honest woman of her!

A pregnant bachelorette, who realizes she cannot take care of a baby alone, may resort to an abortion. She will look for a doctor who will remove the baby from her uterus before it grows big, killing the embryo. Some believe that abortion is an acceptable practice and

that an unborn baby is not really a person in the first few months of pregnancy.

However, the fetus is alive from the moment the sperm joins the egg, and if the fertilized egg is left in peace, it will grow into a complete human being. It is stated implicitly in the Qur'an and explicitly in the Hadith that the fetus is not ensouled until the fourth month. If a woman's unborn baby – from the age of four months – dies for some reason in later pregnancy and she has a miscarriage, the baby must be given a name, buried with respect, and prayed for.

Islam teaches mercy and respect for all human life. Every human being has the right to live (unless s/he has committed certain major crimes like murder, which deserve capital punishment). This is called the right to life and it is the most basic right that the Creator grants everyone. Hence, an abortion in the absence of a good reason is regarded in the same light as murder by most Muslim scholars because it kills a helpless innocent human being.

The only time a woman is permitted to have an abortion is if her own life is in danger if she continues the pregnancy, and, according to some jurists, in cases of rape and incest. Other jurists put such strict limitations only after ensoulment and consider other reasons acceptable during the first four months. Nevertheless, Islam discourages abortion at any time and prohibits abortion beginning in the fourth month. Abortion is allowed for exceptional cases: to avoid a danger to the mother's life, or to avoid grave consequences for the family honor, and to avoid a horrible psychological and social impact on the mother, the baby, and the entire family.

Although abortion is permitted in very few circumstances by some schools of thought, it is not allowed as a means of birth control or avoiding the economic cost of an unplanned pregnancy. If the pregnant girl decides to keep the baby, she will become a single parent of an illegitimate child – a situation that carries tremendous hardship for the unwed mother and the fatherless child.

ADOPTION IN ISLAM

Having done all in their power to prevent extramarital sex, if parents still find themselves with a grandchild in their home, what can they do? Many parents of unmarried pregnant girls often feel deeply ashamed of their daughter's disgraceful behavior and do not want to help take care of a baby born outside of marriage. Islam allows the mother to give up the baby for adoption. Islam encourages adoption as a way to take care of orphans. However, the orphan's wealth must be preserved, as well as knowledge of the orphan's family origins. Unmarried mothers often have to give up their babies for adoption and they may never see their children again. They will always wonder about them, and when the children themselves grow up and realize that they have been adopted, they will be curious about their biological parents and relatives.

Not all children put up for adoption end up in good homes. Some children are never adopted. They are either raised in orphanages or sent from one foster home to another, where they may be mistreated. In some societies, if it is known that a child is illegitimate, he or she is teased and not accepted by others. These children – resentful of the treatment they receive – can often grow up to be troubled children.

Can the adopted child be called by the name of the adopting father? The Qur'an considers lineage a serious issue, and it prohibits any person's true identity to be faked.

…nor has He made your adopted sons your sons. Such is [only] your [manner of] speech by your mouths.
(Qur'an 33:4)

Every human being must be called by the name of his true biological father:

Call them by [the names of] their fathers: that is more just in the sight of Allah. But if you do not know their fathers' [names, call them] your Brothers in Faith, or your mawlās [close friends].
(Qur'an 33:5)

If the biological father is unknown, the Qur'an states that they are your brothers and sisters in religion and close friends, and can receive your family name. The major issue here is not a literal naming only but to confer acceptance and dignity on the children. To confirm the principle of brotherhood, the Prophet ﷺ showed us a practical and dignified example by marrying Zaynab (his cousin) after she was divorced by his previously adopted son, Zayd ibn Hārithah.

> *Then when Zayd had dissolved [his marriage] with her, with the necessary [formality], We joined her in marriage to you: in order that [in the future] there may be no difficulty to the Believers in [the matter of] marriage with the wives of their adopted (claimed) sons, when the latter have dissolved with the necessary [formality] [their marriage] with them.*
>
> (Qur'an 33:37)

One may reflect on the similarity between the malpractice of hiding lineage during the pre-Islamic "Age of Ignorance" and that of the twenty-first century, in which calling adopted children by the adopted father's name is common. These practices need to be stopped and, if known, the true biological name revealed. The most important factor is doing what is best for the orphan and preserving the orphan's rights. The detailed mechanics depend on the prevailing culture and practices at the time.

Homosexuality and Parents

A homosexual is a person who is sexually attracted to members of his own sex, and chooses to have sexual relations with them rather than with the opposite sex. A heterosexual is a person who limits sexual relations to members of the opposite sex. Women who have sex with other women are called lesbians. Gay is a slang word for a homosexual male. We maintain from the outset that our intention is to discuss an issue which has great moral and precious significance for humanity. While we are unequivocally against the act of homosexuality and its promotion, we are not against homosexuals as people because human beings are to be treated with dignity and respect, not hatred. The idea is to help parents whose children feel they are homosexual in a world which scripturally condemns it but which under secular legal systems has given it legitimacy.

The Qur'an and the Holy Books condemn homosexual activity:

> *Of all the people in the world, will you approach males, And leave those whom Allah has created for you to be your mates? Nay, you are a people transgressing [all limits]!*
>
> (Qur'an 26:165–166)

This is an extremely uncomfortable and awkward issue for parents to face. Having performed all their duties correctly as parents, what can mothers and fathers do if suddenly confronted with the discovery that their son is a homosexual? If the teenage son seems to be adopting homosexual tendencies, it is important that his parents tread carefully and seek proper help for him.

Homosexuality is a difficult subject for parents. Some believe the less they know about it, the better. Parents take pride in seeing their sons to be masculine in every respect and their daughters, likewise, feminine. Nevertheless, facts must be faced. There are over

10 million homosexuals in the United States (Smith et al. 2001) and they were all children once; their numbers are on the rise.

Homosexuals have become more and more active in fighting for more rights. They hold parades and protest marches and try to change the laws that limit their freedom. It is possible to see men kissing each other on the lips in public or dressed up as women. The latter are called transvestites or cross-dressers (although most transvestites are heterosexual, the "gay rights" movement has embraced "transgender issues"). In some countries and states, men may even marry men and women may marry women. These homosexual couples want to be treated like normal married couples. Although they cannot have children together, sometimes they adopt children. Anyone daring to condemn their behavior is labeled "homophobic," that is, afraid of homosexuals!

Development of the birth control pill in the U.S. in the 1960s, the legalization of abortion, and the teachings of popular psychology led to what is known as the sexual revolution. People in more liberal societies began to claim that they should be free to have sex with whomever they wished, whether they were married or not, and whether they were the same or the opposite sex, and that they should be respected for their sexual orientation. Many people began to accept these ideas, with the result that today it is against the law in many countries to discriminate against homosexuals.

How does a person become a homosexual? Numerous theories have been proposed. Is it something that one can choose, or is it something one is "born" with and discovers as one grows up? Until the 1970s, homosexuality was viewed by most experts to be a type of mental illness or disorder. The medical profession maintained that certain boys with weak, cruel, and cold mothers could grow up to hate all women, and that certain girls abused by their fathers could grow up to hate all men, explaining why they would then seek to love people of the same sex. In the 1990s some medical and behavioral professionals began developing a theory which claimed that homosexuality was in fact a normal variation of human sexual orientation. They claimed that homosexuality originated in one's genes and is a trait which could be inherited (pointing to some families having more homosexuals than others, although it could equally be argued that this could be due to the way the families were raising their children). In addition, discovering rare cases of certain animals engaged in homosexual behavior, the conclusion was drawn by some that this could also be normal for people; a strange inversion of reasoning, for one should ask the question: are the activities of wild animals to be used as a barometer to define the norm of human action, or a reason to give certain behavior social acceptance? Do people consider animals to be their model of conduct?

Human values are not to be derived from animal behavior. People are different from animals; and God has honored human beings above all other creation.

Some possible reasons for homosexuality are discussed below. Genetics is suggested as one explanation. However, experience, environmental factors, and issues in the formation of relationships have major influence and importance:

- Confusion about friendship: Young people who have strong feelings for a friend of the same sex are sometimes confused by all this talk of homosexuality. They begin to wonder if they, too, are homosexual or lesbian. A girl may be so happy with her best friend that she has an urge to give her a big hug and a kiss. She may feel guilty about those urges, confusing them with sexual feelings. If she becomes convinced that she is a lesbian, she may try to persuade her girlfriend to have sex with her. The solution to this may be that parents should provide an adequate sex education for their children.
- Lack of love for children: A person may not have anyone else to turn to for love and affection. Teenagers who have poor relationships with their parents and relatives need to be touched and loved by someone. If the only friend they have is someone of the same sex, the overwhelming need to touch and hold someone may overcome their sense of decency and lead to sexual acts. The solution is a preventive one, to smother the children with love and affection, starting with breastfeeding in infancy.

Loving relations should continue among all members of the same family, forever. This way, the person finds natural love within the home and does not look for it outside.

- Child molestation: Some young people are taken advantage of by child molesters and pushed into these acts against their will, until they become used to it. In a systematic study of 2881 men who had had sexual relations with other men, Paul et al. (2001) found that one fifth had experienced child sexual molestation. The solution is for parents to keep a continuous watch and check on their youngsters, ensuring that they are always in good company. Be aware that child molesters are often family members and vigilance is paramount.
- Abnormality: Some people are born with or develop rare diseases as a result of which they do not have enough male or female hormones to make them look and behave like normal men and women. Hormones are chemicals produced in various organs of the body that are responsible for physical sex characteristics (such as the growth of female breasts). Hormones also affect characteristics that are masculine (like growing a moustache and beard, developing muscles, the desire to fight and show off) or feminine (like the desire to cuddle babies). A young man without enough male hormones might not be able to grow a beard, his voice might not deepen as it should, and he might not feel masculine inside. The solution may lie with medical treatment.
- Long delays in marriages: Men and women who are deprived of marriage at the proper age may still feel a strong urge to satisfy their sexual desires. If not done

appropriately, alternative ways will creep into their minds. Early marriage is to be encouraged at the legal age, for it is the right of children. It is also the duty of parents to facilitate marriage.

Parents confronted with the discovery that their son has homosexual tendencies need to be patient and understanding, and need to seek professional help immediately. They should not withhold love from their children. Although it may be illegal for individuals to discriminate against homosexuals, they do not have to accept homosexual activity, even if they become unpopular by criticizing it, for we all have the freedom to disagree. Just as the law protects the rights of homosexu-als, it also protects the freedom of religious beliefs.

Parents must be aware of the legal issues related to homosexuality: U.S. law prohibits discrimination on the basis of sex, sexual orientation, race, language or national origin. Many societies are sending the message to children that to be a homosexual is acceptable. These societies are blurring the line between what is normal and what is not.

Children are also being told to ignore their natural inhibitions and to follow their passions.

We encourage parents to make it very clear to children that homosexual behavior is wrong. Parents must also intervene if a teacher encourages homosexual behavior.

Men should be masculine
(respectful toward women, defenders of the weak, not reveal their bodies).
Women should be feminine
(wear modest clothing, lower their gaze, defend their honor against misbehaving men).

Islamic Sex Education

Islam recognizes that the Almighty created sexual need. Sex is discussed with dignity in the Qur'an and by the Prophet ﷺ within the context of marriage and family life. Islam does not treat women (or men) as merely objects of sexual pleasure but considers them with respect in a framework of a complementary relationship that fulfills the human need and the Will of God. Whereas sex outside marriage is wrong and a major punishable sin (scripturally), sex with one's spouse is a virtue rewarded as an act of worship. Islamic laws regarding sex are clear and natural; they do not change with peer pressure or the changing values of society. Virginity at the time of marriage is a virtue, unlike in some societies where it may be a disadvantage.

Sexual relationships between men and women are depicted in the verses below:

> *Did We not create you out of a devalued fluid, which We then let remain in [the womb's] firm secure place for a term pre-ordained? Thus have We determined [the nature of man's creation]: and excellent indeed is Our power to determine [what is to be]!*
> (Qur'an 77: 20–23)

And do not even approach adultery (and fornication) for, behold, it is an abomination and an evil way.

(Qur'an 17:32)

The following are some references from the Sunnah concerning husband and wife relationships:

The Prophet ﷺ considers marital intimacy as a rewardable act of virtue. He says:

"When one of you sleeps with his wife, it is a rewardable act of virtue." The Companions were surprised and said, "How is it that we satisfy our desires and we get rewarded for it?" The Prophet replied, "If one has done it in a forbidden way, it would have been counted as a sin, but if you do it legitimately, it is rewarded." (MUSLIM)

The Prophet ﷺ teaches that intimate acts between spouses are secrets not to be told to others:

"Worst among you on the Day of Judgment is a man who exposes himself to his wife and she exposes herself to him, then he divulges her secrets to others." (MUSLIM)

'Ā'ishah narrates:

While I was lying with the Messenger of Allah ﷺ under a bed cover, I menstruated, so I slipped away and I took up the clothes [which I wore] in menses. Upon this he asked: "Have you menstruated?" I said: "Yes." He called me and I lay down with him under the bed cover. (AL-BUKHĀRĪ AND MUSLIM)

'Ā'ishah reveals how she had slipped graciously from the bed to leave the side of the Prophet ﷺ one night. However, when he found out that it was because she had started her period, he simply told her to cover herself and then lie down with him again. The Prophet ﷺ and his wife 'Ā'ishah used to sleep "together under one cover," as several hadiths confirm. Husbands and wives are described in the Qur'an as garments for each other. A garment is very personal and is close to one's body, so similarly spouses should be very close to each other. A garment protects and shields our modesty, so spouses should also do the same for each other. Garments are put on whenever one wishes, so they should be available to each other for enjoyment at any time. A garment adds to a person's beauty, so they should beautify each other.

Sex is an expression of love, for one without the other is incomplete. The husband's responsibility is to educate his wife in matters of sexuality, especially in his likes and dislikes, and he should not compare her with other women. Wives should do the same to achieve maximum enjoyment. Wives need to realize that men's sexual needs are different from theirs. Instead of being a passive recipient, a wife should try to be an active and loving participant. Both are exposed to serious temptations outside the home, which puts the husband and wife in an unfair situation of continual competition with outside influences. Hence, in the interests of both, she has to be available to please her husband so as not to pressure him or give him an excuse to make a choice between his wife and other women, who lead him to destroy the family and earn the displeasure of God. Similarly, the husband has to be readily available to please and satisfy all the needs of his wife.

The Prophet ﷺ explains in further detail the intimate practices between spouses so that the maximum pleasure is attained. Islam discourages anal sex strongly and there is nothing in the Qur'an or the Sunnah to prohibit oral sex. Sexual organs should be kept clean and a shower (*ghusl*) should be taken after any fluid discharge or sexual intercourse.

The Prophet ﷺ said: "No one of you should fall on his wife like the beast. There should be a [messenger] between spouses. He was asked: "What messenger do you mean?" He said: "The messenger is kissing and talking [foreplay]."

(NARRATED BY AL-ZUBAYDĪ
AND AL-ʿIRĀQĪ)

The Prophet ﷺ also said: "When you sleep with your wife, you must be compassionate [considerate] to her. If you satisfy yourself before she does, you should not rush her until she is fully satisfied."

(ABŪ YAʿLĀ)

Every man has the duty to look after his life partner properly. If he expects her to be faithful to him, then it is his duty to give her sufficient time to achieve full sexual pleasure. It usually takes around 15–20 minutes to satisfy a woman. A man is not supposed to fling himself on his wife like an animal – that is intercourse without sport and foreplay. This is disapproved of in Islam, and men have to be considerate. They need to understand the biological facts of female sexuality, learn techniques to pleasure their wife, and go ahead and enjoy a fulfilled and happy life. Any man who cannot spare his wife this time is causing her distress, as well as placing powerful temptations in her path.

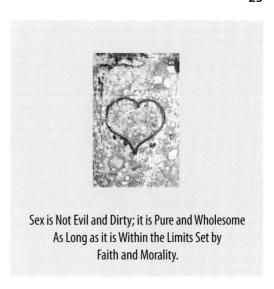

Sex is Not Evil and Dirty; it is Pure and Wholesome As Long as it is Within the Limits Set by Faith and Morality.

Parents' Duty Towards Children

It is important that parents teach their children a positive attitude toward sex: It is not the creation of the Devil, nor is it evil or dirty (if it is dealt with rightly). It is the gift and mercy of the Compassionate, and an insight into some of the joys of Paradise to come.

Although sex is an activity that is so pleasurable and wonderful (as it should be), it is also an opportunity that can be misused by Satan to corrupt, twist, deprive, and cause huge suffering. More suffering is probably caused on earth by sex than by anything else, including famine and war. The risk is so high that by committing one wrong sexual act, one may be obliged to live out one's lifetime in a minefield of endless disasters. Sex is a need that has to be satisfied according to the commands of the Creator in a pure and wholesome manner, without excess, deprivation, and suffering.

The Prophet ﷺ was open, kind, and honest in understanding the needs of men and women. He was not prudish or bigoted, and he himself obviously enjoyed his marriages. This was certainly the view of ʿĀʾishah, who undeniably knew the Prophet ﷺ more intimately than anyone else.

Sexual pleasures must be subject to moral considerations. Permissiveness in sex leads to the breakdown of family and society, to lying and deception, to lack of responsibility, and even to crimes like rape, drug addiction, theft and murder. If one really loves God, then one has to be able to resist temptations responsibly and know right from wrong. Many people are so modest and repressed that they do not try to gain the knowledge of how to practice sex in the most fulfilling way.

Sex and Hygiene: Menstruation, Pubic Hair, Circumcision, Seminal Fluid

SEX DURING MENSTRUATION: Medieval Jewish practice during the monthly period was to avoid contact with women completely. The Prophet ﷺ instructed the Companions to associate fully with their wives during menstruation, though they should avoid penetration and touching the private parts.

Girls need to be given practical advice about how to use sanitary towels and how to dispose of them without clogging the toilet. The alternative is disposable pads/rags, which can be washed, dried and reused. Monthly periods are natural and do not have to be secretive and embarrassing, especially if the daughter needs help because she suffers discomfort or pain.

PUBIC HAIR: The Prophet ﷺ recommended that pubic hair for men and women needs to be removed periodically – once a month – so that the body is kept clean and neat, ready for one's spouse to enjoy. Pubic hair is natural and healthy, and the practice of removing it brings peace of mind and cleanliness.

A boy does not mind developing a hairy chest or legs, or growing a mustache. Many girls however, do not like it. Girls can be horrified to discover long dark hair growing around their nipples, and hate it when their legs and arms become covered in thick dark hair. Mothers can be very useful in showing girls how to use depilatory creams or other means of keeping themselves smooth and attractive. Girls need not worry that they are turning into men if they grow a mustache, or have a few whiskers on their chins. These can either be removed or carefully bleached, if they become a problem. Girls should be comfortable with their body, and should not be obsessed with pleasing men in public.

CIRCUMCISION: The Prophet ﷺ strongly recommended circumcision for boys at an early age. This promotes better hygiene and more sexual enjoyment at marriage. Circumcision for males reduces cancer, decreases infections, and lessens pain during urination. Girls should not be circumcised. Islam prohibits the cutting of any part of the female genitals.

SEMINAL FLUID AND NOCTURNAL EMISSIONS IN BOYS: Some teenagers become highly embarrassed if there is any soiling or discharge on their underwear, and are terrified of their parents seeing it. It is helpful to reassure them that a certain amount of discharge is normal. If it is colored or blood-stained, or smelling, or their underwear needs changing more than once a day, then medical

advice should be sought. Semen is not to be confused with urine. Urine is filthy (*najis*) and must be washed clean. Semen is clean and need not be washed like urine, just cleaning it with a few drops of water and rubbing it should be sufficient.

Teenagers and Abstention

American and Canadian children today are reaching puberty earlier than ever. Girls may enter puberty between the ages of 8 and 13, while boys enter puberty between the ages of 9 and 14. In Britain, over the past 150 years, the average age of puberty has fallen from 16.5 years to 12.8 years. This may be due to the increased consumption of animal products, most of which come from animals intensively reared with regular doses of antibiotics and hormones as growth promoters.

On the other hand the average age for first marriage is rising. In the United States, it is about 29 for men and 26 for women. In Jordan, where the economic situation is different, the average age for marriage is 35 for men and 30 for women. People who believe in abstinence before marriage are asking their children to curb their sexual desires from the time they reach puberty till they get married,

which is a wait of about 16 years, a time during which sexual desire and energy are at their peak. This is a tremendous challenge for young adults.

Up until 100 years ago most people got married soon after puberty. Societies were struggling to survive. Because of high infant mortality and frequent wars, it was important that both men and women married early when their sexual strength and vitality were at their peak.

Some societies have adapted to late marriage by unleashing sexual restraints. Religious people cannot do that, yet their insistence on abstinence is very difficult for teenagers. It does not seem likely that human beings can suppress their sexuality from puberty till marriage (possibly 20 years later). A teenager with screaming hormones is going to suffer in today's environment of continuous temptations all around.

Muslim societies must adopt early marriage to cope with the situation. The ramifications of this alternative could also be problematic. Nevertheless, parents have to find a way to tell their teenagers why sex outside of marriage is forbidden to them, even though they need it urgently. The extended family can help young couples with child-rearing, especially if family

planning is practiced wisely.

Some Muslim scholars have ruled that masturbation should be avoided, except when it becomes a relief from immense sexual desire for bachelors, and it must not become a habit. When the sex urge becomes uncontrollable, masturbation can be a much lesser evil. In his book *Rudūdun ʿalā Abāṭīl*, the late Shaykh Muhammad al-Hamid explains that the jurists prohibit masturbation if it is used to arouse passive sexual desire. However, when the desire is so overwhelming that it occupies the mind and disturbs the stability of the person (to the extent of pushing him/her toward adultery) and if masturbation helps to pacify the compelling urge, then it is permissible. Masturbation can be neutral, earning neither reward nor punishment, neither blame nor praise; it is neither a sin nor a good deed.

Masturbation is self-centered. In isolation, instead of intense intimacy, a teenager can satisfy his fantasy. Although it may be helpful as a temporary escape from tension, for teenagers, however, it can become an easy substitute for marriage. When a teenager's main satisfaction comes from a personal relationship, self-gratification is a problem for him.

Parents should be understanding if their teenagers use masturbation as for sexual tension. Usually, it is gone by the time they mature and get married. The important thing is that parents keep their children busy in playing sports or developing a habit of fasting two days every week, and include them in group activities. They need to inform them that the misuse of masturbation could be a serious health problem and that situations of temptation and sexual pressure have to be avoided. In this way, the teenagers are discouraged from allowing masturbation to become an obsession.

Parents need to be frank with children about how to deal with their bodies. Sex occupies a considerable amount of the young adults' thinking, yet it is the subject that is least likely to be discussed between parents and their children, and when they do address the matter they are not very realistic. Muslim jurists will tell teenagers that masturbation is forbidden, although a few scholars have permitted it with some constraints. Most teenagers will practice it anyway, and live with the perception of shame or guilt. A balance has to be sought and this practice has to be used only as a last resort and even then at a minimum level, without harming the body, physically or emotionally.

The Islamic Solution to the Sexual Dilemma: A Road Map for a Preventive Approach

The basic approach is avoidance: *Lā taqrabū al-zinā*, avoid approaching adultery and fornication. Distance yourselves; do not approach any situation that leads to such a sin.

Nor come near to adultery: for it is a shameful [deed] and an evil, opening the road [to other evils]. (Qur'an 17:32)

The important phrase here is "do not approach" (*Lā taqrabū*): do not come near it; avoid it, shield yourself from it, thus implying that one should block all avenues leading to it, to the extent that it will become practically inaccessible as much as possible. The strategy of society should be preventive, to make it difficult to commit the sin by taking measures to make unlawful sex virtually unavailable and inaccessible. By cutting off all kinds of sex trade, restricting supply, and minimizing demand, society can direct behavior correctly and keep marriages clean and safe. This type of morality is not new or unique to Islam, it was originally taught by other faiths (including Christianity, Judaism, and Hinduism). No sane person thinks that it is a good idea for young or old people to practice a chaotic sexual life and become enslaved to their physical desires. People who believe in God regard the ideal place for sex as within marriage. The problem is that in many societies, this conservative attitude toward sexual practice has been rejected by the younger generations.

Nowadays, the roads leading to sexually transmitted diseases (STDs) are wide open and inviting. Avoiding them demands some sacrifice. The fruits of abstinence are rich,

whereas the agony that results from indulgence in unlawful sexual intercourse is terrible. When the totality of the Islamic system is examined, it is apparent that it is clearly centered on the protection and sanctity of the family. A great emphasis is placed on things such as modesty in the dress code, no sex outside marriage, abstention from alcohol and drugs, no dating, no provocative communication between genders, no unsupervised mixing, no pornography, no vulgar sexual scenes on television, and no sexually arousing advertisements and music. All these are serious efforts to block the roads leading to adultery and fornication. In addition, parents are responsible for explaining to their teenagers the dangers of irresponsible sex.

This preventive approach to avoid *zinā* (illegitimate sexual relationships) should start early in infancy. Both individual and collective efforts are needed to moderate the sexual urge in teenagers.

The Qur'an recognizes the overwhelming sexual desire that can exist in people. Even Prophet Joseph, under the pressure of seduction, would have fallen, had it not been for the Mercy of his Lord Who saved him at the critical moment:

And [it so happened that] she in whose house he was living [conceived a passion for him and] sought to make him yield himself unto her; and she bolted the doors and said, "Come thou unto me!" [But Joseph] answered: "May God preserve me! Behold, goodly has my master made my stay [in this house]! Verily, to no good end come they that do [such] wrong!"

And [with passion] did she desire him, and he would have desired her, but that he saw the evidence of his Lord: thus [did We order] that We might turn away from him [all] evil and shameful deeds: for he was one of Our servants, sincere and purified. (Qur'an 12:23–24)

The God-given sexual urge in men and women is usually dormant, and should not be gratuitously instigated and aroused. Our sexual urges should be satisfied in marriage. If temptation is abundant, lust is awakened early

and it becomes difficult to control. However, sexual arousal in men is more obvious and less controllable than in women and the passage into puberty for boys awakens sexual feelings. Women have greater control over their sexual desires and behavior than men.

The permissive sexual environment that is widely evident in many societies in the twenty-first century is not surprising. Society is doing very little to help the youth; it is in effect throwing teenagers into a lake with their hands tied and telling them: "beware of getting wet!" Temptation inflames the sexual urge in teenagers, whereas society expects them to refrain and impose self-restraint. It is like putting a tasty fish before a hungry cat and telling it "don't eat!" Abstention becomes much easier and achievable in the absence of temptation.

> He tied his hands, then threw him
> in the water, and told him:
> Beware! Beware! Don't get wet!

Man can be sexually aroused easily by touching, seeing, hearing, smelling, or even by pure imagination. It is essential that all the means of temptation, seduction, and arousal are removed as much as possible. It is much wiser to adopt the safe defensive approach by avoiding trouble rather than falling into it and then struggling to get out. Once people are aroused, their defenses are dramatically weakened and the likelihood of giving way to temptation increases.

The Qur'anic approach is preventive and holistic. The question is: How can teenagers maintain desirable ethical standards in a society that is sexually permissive? Is it humanly possible? According to Islamic law, anything that leads to wrongdoing is wrong. Hence, anything which breaks down sexual inhibition and loss of self-control over the body should be avoided.

The following is a list of many steps to block the roads leading to unlawful sex. Reducing temptation is a lifelong process that requires the cooperation of parents, the extended family, the school, the media, and the community.

MODESTY (ḤAYĀ')

It is important to establish the concept of modesty (*Ḥayā'*) from birth by respecting the private parts of the baby. Parents need not touch the baby's genitals except when bathing with hands in a cloth, and for only a short time. Also, the genitals of children aged three years and above have to be covered with a cloth, even during washing. Avoiding the exposure of the genitals augments the personal privacy of the child.

What is modesty? Modesty (*Ḥayā'*) is defined as: "bashfulness," embarrassment, and shyness from any action that degrades the person. In Arabic it means:

> A trait or an attitude that causes a person embarrassment or fear of a scandalous act.

Jurists define modesty as a character trait that discourages a person from committing vices or shameful, filthy acts.

Modesty is a quality that has to be consistently nourished by parents so that it becomes the norm in both family and society. Even in funerals, when washing the dead body, the person(s) doing the cleaning should not stare at the genitalia nor touch them directly by hand, but use a cloth to clean the private parts of the deceased. To realize the extent and dimensions of modesty, the Prophet ﷺ said the following:

> Faith has over seventy branches. The best of them is the saying "there is no God but Allah." The least is the removal of a harmful object from the footpath. And modesty is a branch of faith. (MUSLIM)

What people have inherited from early prophethood is: If you have no shame (*Ḥayā'*), you may do whatever you please. (ABŪ DĀWŪD)

The Prophet ﷺ said:
Obscenity can produce only ugliness. Modesty can produce only goodness and beauty. (IBN MĀJAH)

Al-Jurjānī divides modesty into the following two categories:

a) The psychological part, which is found in all humans, such as not exposing the private parts or not having sexual intercourse in the presence of others. This type of *Ḥayā'* exists in humans, and may be a part of their innate nature; and

b) Modesty acquired from faith, which preserves the individual from committing evils owing to the love of God and fear of His punishment.

Modesty is a branch of faith

Children need to be taught the following acts of modesty:

1. to lower their gaze when looking at the other sex or at an obscene scene;
2. to walk modestly without sexual provocation or imitating the other sex;
3. to talk gently and respectfully without sexy overtones;
4. to dress modestly, covering the body nicely and with dignity.

The following three situations are where modesty is not required:

1. In scholarship: Seek knowledge (the more the better) particularly in religious instructions relating to marital sex, menstruation, pregnancy, and nocturnal emissions. Jurists, within the context of education, have coined the phrase: "There is no embarrassment (shyness) in religious learning." We may extrapolate the same phrase to state: "no embarrassment (shyness) in seeking knowledge."

2. In reform: Promote righteousness and forbid evil, for it is a duty to be discharged firmly and wisely.
3. In marriage: There is no shyness between spouses in their home. The Prophet ﷺ said:

Conceal your private parts except from your spouse. (ABŪ DĀWŪD, IBN MĀJAH, AND AL-ḤĀKIM)

Whereas sex is completely forbidden between non-spouses, it is virtually limitless between spouses in the privacy of their bedroom.

If parents neglect implanting modesty in their children, society will suffer. Modesty is the strong foundation of immunity against temptation and seduction. The following are some observations on the results of a lack of modesty among nations:

- Under the guise of art and free expression, museums and public squares in many countries have become littered with depictions of naked men and women on posters and in naked sculptures, exposing their private parts. This is also found in some temples in India.

Arabic Poetry on Modesty

If you do not fear the consequences of how you behave and you fail to act modestly, you can do whatever you want.

But, by God, there is no goodness in an immodest life! One lives comfortably, as long as one acts modestly; just as a tree trunk stays protected as long as it is covered by bark.

For many there is a clear line between what is considered art and what is considered pornographic or obscene. Nudity in Western artistic traditions is an interesting development primarily because it often purports to be symbolic of virtue, honor, and the glory of man. A good example is Michael Angelo's statue David, a prophet, representing all that is good, sculpted entirely naked. Certain temples across the world (e.g. India) also depict full frontal nudes in a religious setting. Of course the statue of David is really a symbol of Renaissance man and not the prophet as such. The whole subject of the social acceptance and interpretation of nudity is something parents have to think more deeply about, particularly as regards their children.

- In a museum in Santiago, Chile, sculptures of a man and a woman performing sexual intercourse are on display.
- A young woman in the United States had video cameras in her bedroom and bathroom, transmitting live pictures 24 hours a day to viewers over the Internet.
- In the United States, fifty thousand people logged on to watch the first live birth delivery of a child on the Internet in full graphic detail.

(*Time*, June 29, 1998)

Some etiquettes of modesty are listed here:

- As children grow up, they have to knock before entering the bedrooms of parents and other relatives (to avoid the possibility of seeing them undressed or exposed).
- Parents and siblings should cover their bodies and dress respectfully, both inside and outside the home. The use of make-up and sexually attractive cosmetics and perfumes should be avoided. Parents need to watch their language when in the presence of children, avoiding sexual talk. Nor should there be any explicit sexual contact between parents in front of children, including deep kissing, and touching of the private parts.
- When children are 10 years old, they are to sleep in separate beds.
- Boys and girls should be taught to avert their gaze when looking at the opposite sex.

Say to the believing men that they should lower their gaze and guard their modesty: that will make for greater purity for them: and Allah is well acquainted with all that they do. And say to the believing women that they should lower their gaze and guard their modesty; that they should not display their beauty and ornaments except what [must ordinarily] appear thereof; that they should draw their veils over their bosoms and not display their beauty except to their husbands, their fathers, their husbands' fathers, their sons, their husbands' sons, their brothers or their brothers' sons, or their sisters' sons, or their women, or the slaves whom their right hands possess, or male servants free of physical needs, or small children who have no sense of the shame of sex; and that they should not strike their feet in order to draw attention to their hidden ornaments. And O you Believers! Turn all together towards Allah, that you may attain Bliss.

(Qur'an 24:30–31)

Lowering the gaze is essential. The Prophet ﷺ said:

Whoever lowers his gaze away from that which is unlawful for him, Allah will grant joy in his heart. (IBN MASʿŪD)

- Girls should be taught to walk respectfully to avoid sexual attraction. They are not to lift their dress and show off their legs. They are to avoid talking in a sexually inviting way:

... be not too complaisant of speech, lest one in whose heart is a disease should be moved with desire: but speak a speech [that is] just. (Qur'an 33:32)

- Boys and girls should not be allowed to stay late at night outside the home. A reasonable curfew system can be agreed upon between parents and children.
- Certain types of music are damaging, (those that arouse sexual feelings and whose lyrics are shameful). Music may affect mood by activating melatonin, the hormone from the pineal gland in the brain that is turned on by darkness and turned off by flashing light. It is the same gland that has been thought to trigger puberty, and it affects the reproductive cycle and sexual mood. Sexually explicit rock music raises sexual desire. Some hard-rock music contains pornographic words, and children are to be prevented from listening to "pornographic rock." Once children are exposed to this music, they become desensitized to vice.
- Pornography is a menace to children, for it inflames sexual desires to an unbearable level. It has a long-term effect on the thinking of children, making them visualize these vulgar scenes for a long time, and causing them to daydream of sexual acts.
- Pornography debases women into sex objects which exist to satisfy men's lust. If a husband is aroused by anything of this nature, he should satisfy his urge with his own wife. Bachelors cannot do this, so perhaps it is yet another reason to marry early.

A man cannot be blamed for having urges; but he can be blamed if he gives way to them and hurts other people in the process. So many men hurt their wives (without realizing it) by looking admiringly at other women. The images of models and film stars on billboards, magazine covers, and posters can be a big problem. In your mind they stay forever young and lovely, in comparison with real spouses who grow old, fat, and tired. Spouses have to be considerate and kind to each other; one can be old and still remain attractive (with good planning, a healthy diet, and appropriate exercise).

Nowadays, parents have to be aware of the dangers of Internet pornography, dating, and cheap, obscene sex talk. They must supervise their children better and place computers in a public area of the house, not in the isolation of a child's bedroom.

DRESS CODE

Girls and boys need to behave and dress modestly. They must avoid provocative or seductive clothing and they must avoid drawing attention to their physical charms. They should not wear tight clothing to show the outlines of their figures to those outside the immediate family, or wear sexually oriented jewelry. "See-through" clothing for boys and girls is not allowed, and girls are to cover their heads in public. Boys and girls should not engage in cross-dressing. The following hadith clarifies this point:

> Abu Hurayrah said: The Prophet cursed the man who dresses himself to look like a woman, and the woman who dresses herself to look like a man. (ABŪ DĀWŪD)

What children wear is important. The adage "You act as you dress" implies that children are to dress modestly and respectably. People dress differently according to the occasion: for weekly worship, interviews, anniversaries, parties, or sports. They are attempting to blend in, impress, or increase their chances of being accepted within a particular group. Clothes, hairstyles, and jewelry should appear modest. Generally, parents do not like extreme attire exemplifying rebellion. If modest clothes

are used for almost every situation, then the wearer will make a good impression. Clothes, behavior, and styles that do not exceed the limits are considered modest.

As far as possible, parents need to give their daughter approved "choices." There will come an age – it may be as young as two or three years old – when their daughter will have strong opinions about what she wears. She will resist her parents' choices about how she should dress. A peaceful and practical solution is to lay out two or three outfits for her to choose from, so that she feels she is being given a choice.

In schools where all students wear the same outfit (uniform), they may not like it at first, but will soon "forget" about their clothing, so that it no longer becomes an issue. This avoids frustrating discussions and decisions on "what to wear" every morning. Girls should be made aware that although the "provocative" look may appear "cute," it can convey the wrong signal to boys with unwanted consequences.

NO FREE MIXING AND NO *KHALWAH*

Khalwah is a private meeting between a man and a woman in a secluded place behind a closed door, where no one can see them (such as a hotel room or a lonely place in the country). A satanic sexual trap it is essential to prevent *khalwah* at all costs! The Prophet ﷺ gave us ample warning when he said:

> Whenever a man and a woman are alone in a secluded place, the Devil is their third party. (AL-TIRMIDHĪ)

Free mixing of boys and girls is to be avoided, but mixing supervised by parents and closely watched within the limits of decency and in a controlled atmosphere is allowed. A boy may become attracted to a girl while seeing her regularly at a mosque, a school, a library, or in the market. He might approach her and start an innocent conversation to see if she is interested in him. After talking with each other, they might make a date to meet at a more private place, such as in the park or in a home. With no one watching them, he might dare to touch or kiss her. If she allows him to do that, before long, he will become bold enough to go further. It could end in their having sex without really planning to do so, which could lead to disaster.

> **The Trap !**
>
> Eye Contact → Smile of Approval → Greetings → Chatting → Meeting → Touching → Arousal → Path of No Return → Sin of Sex → Problems!! The results may include STD, pregnancy, abortion, or an illegitimate child.

The above rule should never be relaxed because it is a sure prescription for disaster to happen. Even for highly religious people, it is a strong invitation to evil. All human beings are made of flesh and emotions: even Prophet Joseph had to face this challenge.

- Dating: The dating system is a 'sex gate' for teenagers. It normally brings pain and suffering for the individuals concerned, their families, and their societies. In a 1999 study conducted in the United States, 25 percent of a sample of male college freshmen said that, if on a date they have paid for the dinner and the girl does not 'go all the way,' the boy has the right to force sex on her. Many of these 'date rapes' are not reported (Norris et al. 1999; Bohmer 1993). Anything that

breaks down sexual inhibition and leads to loss of self-control, such as alcohol, drugs, sexually exciting music, petting, or *khalwah*, is not to be allowed. Kissing and petting prepare the body for sex, where the body can be brought to a "point of no return." Dating and sexual freedom harms marriage. The assumption that the couple that has "tried each other out" and so will "know" each other much better is unfounded. Any society that allows these freedoms suffers from unstable families and high rates of divorce.

PEER PRESSURE AND OTHER FACTORS

- There are many reasons why children become involved in sex, the most common of which is peer pressure. Their rationale is that everybody is doing it. Other reasons for pre-marital sex are their desire for being considered competent by adults and as a way to social advancement. For some, it stems from a lack of self-esteem, which they hope to improve by becoming a father or mother. Sometimes, it is due to a lack of other options to divert their sexual energies. Lack of love and lack of appreciation at home can be a factor, whereby detachment from home can lead to attachment elsewhere. The sexual temptation is prevalent everywhere, primarily from magazines, from peers, and from television. In the U.S. about 20,000 sexual scenes are broadcast annually in advertisements, soap operas, prime time shows, and MTV. Parents must therefore flood their children with love, occupy their children's time with useful activities, and practice open communication with their children.
- Intoxicants: Alcohol and drugs are harmful because they reduce self-control and

remove inhibitions from indulging in sex.

- Dancing (which is mixed and involves inappropriate touching between boys and girls) and physical touching between the genders must be avoided, including kissing, petting, necking, massaging, rubbing, and hugging. All these actions arouse sexual urges in the body, bringing it a step nearer to sexual intercourse.

One definition of Dancing with the Opposite Sex is:

Dancing is
Our Vertical Expression of
Our Horizontal Desire!

WHAT TO DO

Parents have to give their children good advice. Parents are not to confine their role to providing shelter, food, clothing, and material needs for their children, but must simultaneously provide spiritual and moral guidance.

- Parents need to fill children's brains with "good thinking" and occupy them with moral and intellectual "food for thought." Higher causes and values have to be all over the menu. One model of advice is how the Prophet ﷺ spoke to a young man who asked him permission for fornication because he could not control his

sexual urges. The Prophet ﷺ reasoned with him by asking if he would approve of someone having sex with his mother, sister, daughter, aunt, or wife. Each time the man answered "no." Therefore, the Prophet ﷺ replied that the woman with whom the young man wanted to have sex was surely somebody's mother, sister, daughter, aunt or wife. The man understood and repented, and the Prophet ﷺ prayed for his forgiveness.

- It is important to strengthen one's sense of identity and avoid being pushed into following the crowd! Parents can achieve this in their children by teaching them a distinct value system, a world view, and a certain code of life. In this way children will remind themselves not to drink alcohol, eat pork, take drugs, or engage in pre-marital sex. Parents themselves should not seek extramarital affairs, for they have to be good examples to their children.

EARLY MARRIAGE

No fixed age is set for marriage. It is becoming fashionable for young men to marry after obtaining a university degree, finding a job, or reaching the age of 26 or more. Similarly, young girls say that they want to marry after the age of 24, declaring, "I am not ready for it." Although they do have normal sexual organs and desires, young people have to realize that they only have two legitimate choices: marry or abstain from sexual intimacy until marriage.

The Qur'an says:

Let those who do not find the means to marry keep chaste until Allah makes them free from want out of His Grace.

(Qur'an 24:33)

> The Prophet ﷺ said:
>
> By God, I am the most pious among you, but I fast and break the fast, I pray and sleep at night, and I marry women. He who rejects my tradition is not of me. (AL-BUKHĀRĪ)
>
> Marriage is half of the religion; the other half is fearing Allah.
> (AL-ṬABARĀNĪ AND AL-ḤĀKIM)

The Prophet ﷺ said:

Those of you young people who have the means should marry, otherwise you should keep fasting, for it curbs desires. (AL-BUKHĀRĪ)

When a boy or a girl feels the strong urge to get married and s/he cannot wait, parents have to try their best to get them married. If they do not, they are pushing their child toward evil in one way or another. One of the duties of parents is outlined by the Prophet ﷺ:

The one to whom a child is given by Allah, should give him/her three rights: a beautiful name, an education, and when s/he attains puberty, he should see to it that s/he is married. (Tibrizi 1985)

If the parents do not heed the child's request and fail to arrange the marriage, the responsibility of sin will also lie with the parents. However, it is equally important not to force young people into marriage. Some parents engage in wrongdoing by forcing marriage partners upon their children. They simply decide that their offspring should marry available family members without giving their children freedom of choice. They deprive them of their rights to see and know their future spouses beforehand. On the other hand, a sensibly arranged marriage with the active participation as well as the approval of the boy and girl is a duty of the parents, because this will result in a happy lasting relationship between the couple and the two families. These "arrangements" need to have as their objective the happiness and well-being of the couple rather than the selfish motives of the family agents making the arrangements.

The community has several roles to play to facilitate marriage:

- To provide a healthy environment for boys and girls to meet and know each other, while discouraging free unsupervised mixing of the sexes.
- To offer premarital education courses and counseling to boys and girls, and to prepare them for their roles as fathers and husbands and mothers and wives.

The Dilemma of the Educational System vs. Early Marriage

Our current school system has given birth to a complex sexual problem. Obtaining a college or advanced degree dictates that marriage has to be delayed till the mid-twenties. Yet the peak of sexual urge for men is during the late teens; and young women in their late teens have a strong sense of emotional dependency that makes them vulnerable to seduction. Premarital sex during early adulthood results in abortion, unwed mothers, sexually transmitted diseases, and children having illegitimate children.

The solution may seem to be either early marriage during school years or abstinence until graduation from college. Early marriage can be a satisfactory solution if the society prepares teenagers to manage a spouse, and maybe children, responsibly enough.

In modern societies, to demand from teenagers to be patient and remain virgin till the mid-twenties is very difficult nowadays in the midst of temptation and continual sexual provocation. History provides a good lesson. In the past, this problem did not arise because early marriage was the norm and the social network was designed to support that. At the time of the Prophet ﷺ and many centuries later, the following integrated system was implemented:

a) Early marriage was encouraged.

b) The extended family was a great help in taking care of children and grandchildren. It was common to have three generations living closely together and the nuclear family was the exception. Families were much less mobile than today.

c) Islam allowed birth control and population planning to help very young mothers delay pregnancies until they became ready. That depended on the cooperation of the husband and the knowledge of both husband and wife.

Nowadays, mothers who have a profession or hold a university degree can raise children full-time and may have a part time job until their mid-thirties, and then they can work full-time or part-time after their children attain puberty, whether they work as volunteers or for pay. There will be no harm to young children and the society will not be deprived of competent professional mothers with a wealth of experience and wisdom.

It is not right to regard children between the ages of 13 and 19 as incompetent and treat them merely as consumers, devoid of responsibility and productivity. The contemporary trend seems to extend the childhood phase to the early 20's. The youth depend entirely on others instead of being responsible, autonomous, and productive human beings.

The Qur'an speaks of young prophets such as Abraham, Joseph, Moses, and Jesus (peace be upon them all) and others who are meant to be our role models and who accomplished great tasks during their teenage years. There is also the story of the People of the Cave (Aṣḥāb al-Kahf) being young (fityah), rightly guided, and blessed with achievements.

The current model of delaying marriage until the mid-twenties is not satisfactory. Other successful systems of early marriages have been practiced all over the world in the past. Medically speaking, pregnancies and deliveries are easier at a young age and are not at their best during the late twenties or early thirties (and first pregnancies become more difficult with advancing age).

The issue is serious, relevant, and urgent. We must deal effectively with the dilemma of the hardship of sexual restraint, the necessity of early marriage, and the need for establishing a family during the teenage years (to be planned with or without children).

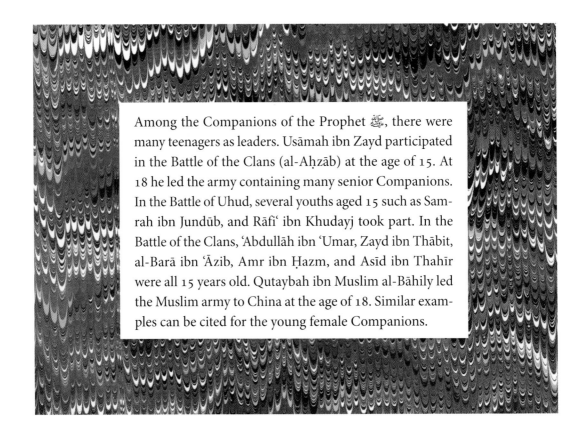

Among the Companions of the Prophet ﷺ, there were many teenagers as leaders. Usāmah ibn Zayd participated in the Battle of the Clans (al-Aḥzāb) at the age of 15. At 18 he led the army containing many senior Companions. In the Battle of Uhud, several youths aged 15 such as Samrah ibn Jundūb, and Rāfiʿ ibn Khudayj took part. In the Battle of the Clans, ʿAbdullāh ibn ʿUmar, Zayd ibn Thābit, al-Barā ibn ʿĀzib, Amr ibn Ḥazm, and Asīd ibn Thahīr were all 15 years old. Qutaybah ibn Muslim al-Bāhily led the Muslim army to China at the age of 18. Similar examples can be cited for the young female Companions.

The Immoral Way	Consequences		The Moral Way	Consequences
Adultery is Easy, Attractive and Available	STD Teenage pregnancy Abortion Unwed Children Having Children Poverty		Do Not Approach Adultery (Zinā)	Healthy parents Healthy children Two-parent homes Leaders of the righteous
Sex is Cheap, Resulting in Irresponsible sex	Divorce Broken homes Single-parent families Sexual chaos High crime rate Higher Incidence of rape	**VS.**	Adultery is Made Difficult, Unattractive and Unavailable Clean sex is dignified Sex is organized through marriage Responsible sex is encouraged	Low crime rate Happy family Happy children Less rape in society

Protecting Children from Sexual Abuse by Adults

It is natural for children to trust adults, and Muslim children, in particular, are trained to obey their elders. Children will be scared if they do not do what an older person asks. Rough adults can be especially scary and intimidating, although if children know what to do, they can protect themselves against abuse. Here are some tips to convey to children against evil adults:

- If a stranger is acting strangely, coming too close, staring, blocking your way, or following you, run away and look for help. If you are sure that he is after you, you can shout "Fire! Fire!" because people usually come right away and it confuses the attacker.
- Never get into a car or go anywhere with a stranger. Even if he seems friendly and knows a lot about you and your parents' name, your school or your address, do not be afraid to say "No!" loudly.

- Avoid deserted places and unsafe neighborhoods, and do not walk alone if you can help it, especially in big cities. It is best for girls to walk to school in groups, or accompanied by an adult.
- Memorize the emergency number for the police, and know how to dial it, even in the dark. Carry coins, tokens, cell phone, or a telephone card at all times to call your parents or the police.
- If you must wait inside a car or at home alone, keep the doors and windows locked. If strangers call at the door or by telephone, do not let them know that you are alone. Never give a stranger your address or any other information over the telephone! Say that your parents cannot come to the door or the phone because they are busy, or that they do not want to be disturbed. Pretend to speak with someone else in the room.
- If you feel uncomfortable about how someone has been looking at or talking to you, tell an older person whom you trust.

- Learn some form of martial arts or self-defense techniques. You do not have to be strong to protect yourself, but simply think smart and act quickly. There are self-defense classes where the emphasis is not on fighting, but on self-defense.
- Be aware of child pornography. Children should never be seen naked before others. The law in many countries restricts pornography, and child pornography is forbidden almost everywhere.
- If you are afraid of someone, recite the Qur'anic chapters of protection (al-Fātiḥah, the kursī verses, al-Falaq, and al-Nās). Keep repeating them if necessary, and make a supplication asking God for help. Allah is your best friend, Guide, and Protector.

AGE APPROPRIATE CHILDREN BE MADE AWARE ABOUT PROSTITUTION

Prostitution is a sex education topic that parents should explain to children if the context arises, taking of course account of their age. Children are not fully aware of the reality of prostitutes' lives and may have questions about them. This should also hinder those who for whatever circumstances may think of leaving home as a way out in the future. Parents are to use their professional and moral judgement. It is important that parents explain to their children the terrible details of a prostitute's life to prevent a casual attitude to sexual relations developing whilst taking account of a child's natural sense of modesty. She may be forced to have painful sex with up to twenty men every day, often contracting serious diseases (such as AIDS), dying at an early age. Very few unlucky girls choose to be prostitutes. Usually they are forced into it by evil men and miserable circumstances. Often they have had to leave their homes because of repeated beatings or sexual abuse, or are drug addicts who need the money to support their expensive habit. Some have been kidnapped when traveling alone, and are kept locked up in rooms in foreign countries where they do not speak the language and do not know how to seek help. They may never see their families again. Others have been drugged during an interview for an apparently respectable job such as a maid or a nanny. They are then stripped of all their belongings, smuggled into another country and kept in a locked room. "At least 4,000 prostitutes in Britain have been trafficked. Anti-trafficking groups say the true figure is much higher" (Morris 2008). In some cases, young girls run away from home owing to an unbearably depressing atmosphere there which feels like hell, seeking comfort outside their home. This is where pimps (men who control prostitutes and sell their services) pick them up and force them into prostitution. Only some of the money paid by customers goes to the girls with the rest going into the pockets of pimps. When parents make life miserable for their children, they are practically pushing them to escape the tortuous conditions of home and take to the streets.

Any child who has serious problems at home and does not know what to do about the situation should seek help from a trustworthy adult (such as a relative, an imam, teacher, counselor or police officer). Running away or turning to drugs to try to escape one's problems will only make things worse.

If children do not know anything about prostitution, they will concoct mental images and start fantasizing. They may think it to be nice, cool, and full of sexual pleasures. Or that it is a profitable profession, having all the cosmetics/perfume they dream of, wearing attractive clothing, causing many men to run after them, or living in 5-star hotels. All these illusions can capture their minds unless parents responsibly explain the facts to them early enough. Unfortunately, the media promote the "exciting" lives of courtesans in history who extracted a luxurious lifestyle out of

wealthy men. Emma Hamilton, the mistress of Horatio Nelson, is an example.

WHEN ONE'S CHILD IS A VICTIM OF INCEST OR RAPE

It is very difficult for a parent to accept that another family member has taken advantage of a younger person by committing incest. Sometimes, it is hard to prove and s/he may not believe it or may not want to believe it. In that case, it is best to go to the imam, a teacher, a counselor, or the police. If a crime has been committed, the police must be informed. Everyone has the right to be safe and protected, and not to be forced into sinful sexual contact.

Rape has become more common today; one out of every four women in the United States is raped at least once in her lifetime. It should also be mentioned that rape victims include children of both sexes, some of them very young. Elderly ladies are also raped by male intruders breaking into their homes.

The following are two examples: "A Saudi court has ruled that a man convicted of raping 5 children will be beheaded." The youngest victim was a boy of 3, left stranded in the desert to die. (BBC News 2009)

London police arrested a man for more than 100 attacks on elderly people (aged from 68 to 93). Known as the "Night Stalker" most of his victims were women and many of the attacks included sexual assault and rape. (BBC News 2009)

If a girl has been raped, she can feel hurt, powerless, angry, and confused. She might feel guilty, thinking that she did something wrong which made the man want to rape her (which is usually not true). Or she might feel deeply ashamed and scared to tell anyone. Any girl who is raped should immediately contact the police, and seek medical help and counselling. This is important because if she

becomes pregnant or contracts a disease from the rapist, a doctor will be able to prove that she was a victim of rape and did not simply have sex with a boyfriend. This is the practical way in which she can clear her name from the accusation of adultery. If a girl is attacked, she should try to run away, or try to dig her fingernails into her attacker. Later, the police might be able to trace the DNA in the tiny bits of skin left under her fingernails to identify the rapist. Screaming may *not* be advisable during the act, for it causes the attacker to panic and he then strangles or suffocates his victim to shut her up; many women and children found murdered have been strangled or suffocated. Although screaming might attract spectators, it is unlikely to attract helpers. It is better to carry a personal alarm, switch it on and, if possible, throw it (or some other object) through the nearest window. Vandalism is guaranteed to make the occupants of the building call the police. Then, if possible before escaping, one should grab something, however small – even a button or a few hairs – of the attacker to help the police identify him. It helps to wear clothes and shoes in which one can run if necessary, such as trousers and walking-shoes. Teenagers have to be made fully aware of date rape and drug rape. These drugs can be administered in non-alcoholic as well as alcoholic drinks.

Counseling must be provided for abuse victims. The counselor can help the victim come to terms with the shock, anger, despair, fear, and disturbing emotions and feelings which the victim will experience.

A Curriculum for Islamic Sex Education

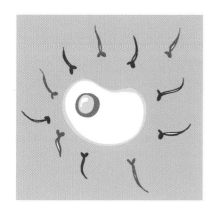

Islamic sex education has to be taught at home, starting at an early age. Before educating about anatomy and physiology, the belief in the Creator needs to be well established. Without a God-fearing belief, certain types of behavior will be thought to be permissible to satisfy lust and desire. The father should teach his son and the mother should teach her daughter. In the absence of a willing parent, the next best choice is a male teacher for boys and a female teacher for girls (preferably a physician or a nurse) at the Sunday Islamic school. The curriculum is to be tailored according to the age of the child, and boys and girls should be taught separately. Only pertinent answers to a question should be given. For example, if a six year old asks, "How did I get into Mom's tummy?" there is no need to describe the whole act. Similarly, it is not necessary to tell a six year old how to put on condoms. This might be taught in a premarital class before marriage.

The curriculum for sex education (Athar 1990) includes:

Qur'anic verses and Prophetic Hadith

Sexual growth and development
Timetable for puberty
Physical changes during puberty
Mental, emotional, and social aspects of puberty

Physiology of the reproductive system
For girls: organs, menstruation, premenstrual syndrome
For boys: organs, the sex drive

Conception, development of the fetus, and birth
Sexually transmitted diseases
Social, moral, and religious ethics
How to resist peer pressure

It is crucial to give sex education to children; otherwise, they will learn wrong information from peers and the media. However, this has to be done in an indirect way. The explicit sexual explanations and removal of all screens between parents and children may be counter-productive. Teach children the physical differences between genders, the right conduct, and the sexual practices that are essential for a healthy Islamic life.

The different roles and objectives of men and women have to be explained in a clear way, according to the phases of development of the child. It is particularly important that parents emphasize the dangers of deviant peers. They should show distaste for improper behavior, and watch carefully for any such inclination in their children. They have to show children how to detect and avoid wrong behavior, and guide children in a practical way toward sexual health.

It is the parents' duty to ensure and facilitate contacts with good peers. Parents of teenagers should not leave them ignorant about proper sexual conduct. Parents have to prevent children from staying out late at night, and prohibit sleepovers when teenagers of the opposite sex are present except when there are trusted adults present and capable of close supervision.

Suggested ages for discussion between parents and children about sex are as follows:

- 5 years old: discuss physical differences between boys and girls
- 10 years old: discuss puberty, seminal fluid, and menstruation
- 15 years old: discuss contraception

[*Note*: Husband and wife team, Dr. Mohamed Rida Beshir and Dr. Ekram, with their two daughters Sumayah and Huda, have authored around 15 books on parenting and family matters both in English and other languages. They also have an extensive website readers may benefit from: www.familydawn.com].

Activities

ACTIVITY 1: ENRICH THE BRAINS OF YOUR CHILDREN!

Benjamin Franklin used to invite a guest for dinner with his family and engage in an intellectual conversation so that his children would hear the conversation and benefit from it without the children being aware that they were the real audience (Franklin 1909). Parents can invite such guests from within or outside the community and ask them in advance to slip certain topics into the conversation to benefit the children.

ACTIVITY 2: A GOOD DEED CHART SYSTEM FOR CHILDREN

> *And be constant in praying at the beginning and the end of the day, as well as during the early watches of the night: for, verily, good deeds drive away evil deeds: this is a reminder to all who bear [God] in mind.* (Qur'an 11:114)

> The Prophet ﷺ said: "Be God-conscious wherever you are, and follow up a bad deed with a good one to wipe it out, and behave well towards people."
>
> (AL-TIRMIDHĪ)

Parents could hang on the refrigerator a chart with each child's name, having three columns: "Extra Credit," "Good," and "Bad." When the children do as they are told, a check mark √ is inserted under the "Good" column, and if a mistake is made, an X is inserted under the "Bad" column. If they do good without being told, they are awarded 2 √ under "Extra Credit." The credit is awarded even if the children do good without the parents' presence (such as at school, or at relatives' or friends' homes); the children report the good deed to the parents, who have to trust them. The points are counted each week and each child is rewarded accordingly. If the checks outnumber the X's, then the child is given a prize (an inexpensive item). If the X's outnumber the checks, then there is no reward. If the child does not earn any prize, s/he will be encouraged to do better next time. It might take more than a week to earn a reward. It is important to check the "Good" column, even if the good deed is small, to motivate and teach children that even the tiniest good deed will make a difference. Although children should not be taught to do good just for the reward, this method helps to instill the right attitude when they are young and they appreciate tangible things (such as small gifts and words of recognition) more than abstract concepts. Parents should also explain to their children that their behavior is what is 'good' or 'bad'. The children themselves are not labelled good or bad; only their behavior is being labelled as such.

EXAMPLE OF A GOOD DEEDS/BAD DEEDS CHART

Hiba

	EXTRA CREDIT	GOOD	BAD
Monday	√√ (helped sister carry backpack)	√ (took out the garbage)	
Tuesday		√ (did her prayers)	X (loud voice)
Wednesday			X (threw trash on the floor)
Thursday		√ (helped teacher carry supplies)	
Friday	√√ (excellent report card)		
Saturday			
Sunday		√ (memorised Qur'an)	
Total	8 √		2 X
Balance	6 √ (gets prize)		

Hala

	EXTRA CREDIT	GOOD	BAD
Monday		√ (made her bed)	
Tuesday			X (hit her sister)
Wednesday	√√ (helped grandma put on socks)		
Thursday		√ (organized her clothes)	
Friday			
Saturday		√ (finished her food)	
Sunday			
Total		5 √	1 X
Balance		4 √ (gets prize)	

Bibliography

Abel, Gene; Harlow, Nora. *The Stop Child Molestation Book*. La Vergne, Tennessee: Ingram Content Group, 2001.

Aids Education Global Information System (AEGIS), (website article dated August 31, 2001). http://www.aegis.com/news/afp/2001/af010886.html

Athar, Shahid. "Sex Education for Muslim Youth and Their Parents." *Journal of Islamic Medical Association (JIMA)*, vol. 22, USA, 1990. —— (editor) *Sex Education: An Islamic Perspective*. http://www.teachislam.com/dmdocuments/33/BOOK/

Bohmer, Carol; Parrot, Andrea. *Sexual Assault on Campus: The Problem and the Solution*. New York: Lexington Books, 1993.

Cancer Research UK. http://info.cancerresearchuk.org/cancerstats/types/cervix/riskfactors/

D'Oyen, Fatima M. *The Miracle of Life*. Leicester, UK: Islamic Foundation, 1996.

Faber, Adele and Elaine Mazlish. *How to Talk so Kids Will Listen & Listen so Kids Will Talk*. New York: Avon Books. 1982.

Institute of Medicine. *The Hidden Epidemic. Confronting Sexually Transmitted Diseases*. Washington, DC: National Academy Press, 1997.

Morris, Sophie. "Sex for sale: The truth about prostitution in Britain." *The Independent*. 26 November 2008.

Norris, Jeannette; Nurius, Paula; Graham, Thomas. "When a Date Changes from Fun to Dangerous." *Violence Against Women*, vol. 5, no. 3, pp. 230-250, March 1999.

Paul, J. P.; Catania, J.; Pollack, L.; & Stall, R. "Understanding Childhood Sexual Abuse as a Predictor of Sexual Risk-taking Among Men who have Sex with Men." *Child Abuse & Neglect*, vol. 25, issue 4, April 2001, pp. 557-584.

Smith, David; Gates, Gary. *Gay and Lesbian Families in the United States*. Washington, DC: Human Rights Campaign, 2001.

Time, June 29, 1998. Giving Birth Online. http://www.time.com/time/community/transcripts/chattr061798.html

Weiss, Rick. "Study Debunks Theory On Teen Sex, Delinquency." *The Washington Post*. Nov 11, 2007. p. A.3